ENDPAPER MAP
POLITECTONIC ZONES

Ray S. Cline

*World Power Trends and
U.S. Foreign Policy
for the 1980s*

Westview Press
Boulder, Colorado

Politecton

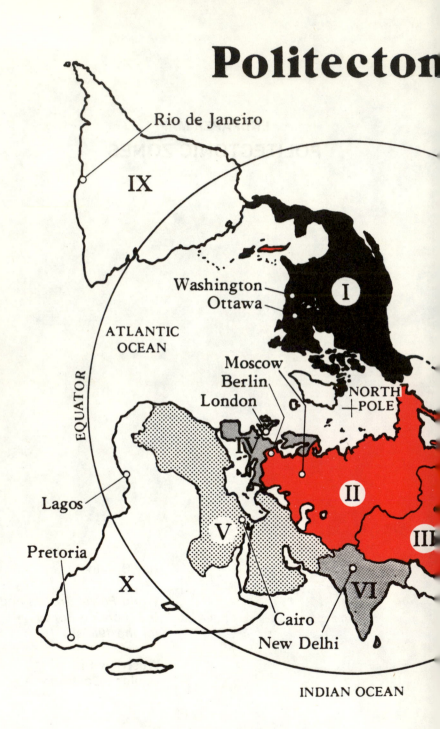

zones

I - North America, Central America
II - USSR, East Europe, Cuba
III - China(PRC), North Korea, Indochina
IV - West Europe
V - North Africa, Mideast
VI - South Asia
VII - Southeast Asia
VIII - Northeast Asia
IX - South America
X - Central and Southern Africa
XI - Australia, New Zealand

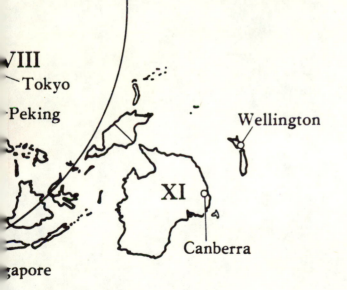

VIII
Tokyo
Peking
Wellington
XI
Canberra
apore

World Power Trends and U.S. Foreign Policy for the 1980s

World Power Trends and U.S. Foreign Policy for the 1980s

Ray S. Cline

Westview Press / Boulder, Colorado

Published in cooperation with The Center for Strategic and International Studies, Georgetown University, Washington, D.C.

Published in 1980 in the United States of America by
  Westview Press, Inc.
  5500 Central Avenue
  Boulder, Colorado 80301
  Frederick A. Praeger, Publisher

Library of Congress Cataloging in Publication Data
Cline, Ray S.
  World power trends and U.S. foreign policy for the 1980s.
  Edition of 1977 published under title: World power assessment 1977.
  1. International relations. 2. Alliances. 3. World politics – 1945- 4. United States – Foreign relations. I. Title.
JX1395.C576   1980   327'.09047   79-26790
ISBN 0-89158-917-1
ISBN 0-89158-790-X pbk.

President Franklin D. Roosevelt's instruction to his speech writer for a fireside chat delivered over the radio six weeks after the Japanese attack on Pearl Harbor, December 7, 1941:

> I'm going to ask the American people to take out their maps. I'm going to speak about strange places that many of them never heard of — places that are now the battleground for civilization. I'm going to ask the newspapers to print maps of the whole world. I want to explain to the people something about geography — what our problem is and what the over-all strategy of this war has to be. I want to tell it to them in simple terms of ABC so that they will understand what is going on and how each battle fits into the picture. I want to explain this war in laymen's language; if they understand the problem and what we are driving at, I am sure that they can take any kind of bad news right on the chin.

Rosenman, Samuel I. *Working with Roosevelt.*
New York: Harper & Brothers, 1952, p. 330.

Contents

PART II
ASSESSMENT OF THE POWER OF NATIONS

PART III
U.S. GRAND STRATEGY
AND FOREIGN POLICY FOR THE 1980s

Tables

Illustrations

Foreword

Most scholars and statesmen agree that the early 1980s promise to usher in an era of strategic instability and peril for the Free World. The United States clearly must act firmly within the context of a coherent defense and foreign policy if it is to maintain an international environment safe for Americans and American allies.

In this troubled era, clearheaded evaluation of strategic trends in all parts of the world is crucial. Realistically assessing the strength of nations and successive tilts in the balance of world power has been the main thrust of the work that Dr. Ray S. Cline has been doing for the Georgetown University Center for Strategic and International Studies (CSIS) during the past five years. His experience as Director of Intelligence and Research in the Department of State (1969–1973) and, before that, Deputy Director of Intelligence for the Central Intelligence Agency (CIA) enables him to put together a uniquely comprehensive and authoritative survey of the main elements of national power. He not only analyzes technical military and economic data but makes qualitative judgments about the geopolitical and foreign policy factors that are fundamental in strategic decisions.

This year the Georgetown Center is proud to present the third, updated assessment by Dr. Cline. His previously published work has become standard teaching material in graduate schools and defense research institutions. One enthusiastic reviewer went so far as to say that the formula for measuring perceived power in the international arena, $P_p = (C + E + M) \times (S + W)$, is the geopolitical equivalent of Einstein's famous nuclear energy formula, $E = mc^2$! The new assessment with strategic recommendations for the 1980s refines the treatment of data in Dr. Cline's formula and draws far-reaching policy conclusions from his analysis of the international balance of power.

This third assessment of world power by Dr. Cline is especially provocative and timely because it delineates and explains worldwide perceptions of a decline in the strength and influence of the United States as compared with the Soviet Union. In many ways this book is the centerpiece of the CSIS study of the many turbulent situations confronting us in the 1980s, and I commend it to all serious observers of international affairs.

David M. Abshire
Chairman, CSIS

Preface

My fervent hope in writing this third comprehensive
assessment of the world power balance is that it will
stimulate sober and realistic thinking about American
defense and foreign policy. It is especially important for
university teachers and students to examine systematically
the geopolitical structure of international conflicts, something too often neglected in intellectual circles in the United
States. Perhaps my formula for combining all the elements
of national power in the simple ways they are perceived by
strategic decision makers will help readers understand the
special challenges confronting Americans in the 1980s.

I deeply appreciate the enormous contribution made to the
completion of this book by my highly professional chief
research editor, who is my wife, Marjorie W. Cline. If strict
justice were done, she would appear as coauthor.

The next greatest debt of gratitude is due to Lieutenant Colonel Harry Wilson, a research associate on loan from the
U.S. Air Force, who compiled many of the statistics and
wisely suggested reorganizing some parts of the text as compared with previous versions. Some of the latest data was
searched out and a great deal of last-minute calculation was
done by my student research assistant, John Panulas.

Ronald Blais performed in an outstanding fashion in
preparing the final text of the manuscript including the

wretchedly complex tables. Finally, I am grateful to my ever dutiful principal secretary, Ann Campagna, my East Asia research associate, Robert Downen, and my special maritime affairs research assistant, Dr. Dora Alves, for the many tasks they helpfully undertook to assist in the course of completing the research and writing of this volume.

I cannot conclude these acknowledgments without thanking all of my colleagues at the Georgetown University Center for Strategic and International Studies for discussing with me over the years the hard problems of strategic analysis that had to be tackled in this impossibly ambitious effort to wrap up everything in a single global assessment of world power.

Washington, D.C.   *Ray S. Cline*

Introduction

This book is my third attempt to assess the power of nations in the international context as a basis for planning American defense and foreign policy. It suggests a realistic way of thinking about the balance of power in the 1980s. In writing *World Power Assessment* in 1975 and in preparing a substantial revision in 1977, I tried to provide a conceptual framework for the comprehensive assessment of national power that would integrate the major geographic, economic, military, and political factors in accordance with the leverage they are commonly perceived to exert in international affairs. This interdisciplinary approach is unique in systematically examining the major power elements it identifies, while measuring them on an overall scale showing specific strengths and weaknesses of nations.

Developing the intellectual framework without applying it as realistically as possible to current problems would have been a sterile effort. As with most theories, it is in application to the real world that insights and approaches are most meaningful. Many factors included in these calculations are necessarily subjective, and the quantitative data are selected only to give broad-gauge measurements that permit simple arithmetical presentation of analytical findings. The data collected for the assessments are not the product of original research; all have been taken from other sources, the most reliable I could find. What is original is the formula for methodically

1

examining and weighing relative levels of perceived power.

This 1980 version is based mainly on information accumulated and consolidated to cover the calendar years 1978 and 1979. Exceptions are noted. To my regret, refinements in methods of quantifications and inclusion of new types of data make this volume not exactly comparable to either my 1975 or my 1977 publication. The basic framework and intellectual approach is identical but the detailed listings and system of weights are different.

In the real world, as in these assessments, the actions of decision makers are based on perceptions of uneven and imperfect knowledge derived from different sources and time frames. Policy cannot await finalized data. Decision makers necessarily must act on the basis of preliminary information and rough estimates. Their perceptions are often not derived from accurate up-to-the-minute data, but from the inexact findings currently available to them. I have tried to keep the best of both worlds by providing fairly "hard" data, yet moving as close to current circumstances as near-term estimates permit. The summary evaluations are very similar to the information base that policymaking officials use to form their perceptions and make their decisions. In any case, the reader will be able to judge the sources cited, arrive at his own conclusions, and supply corrective adjustments when later or better information is available.

The main contribution of this volume, then, is its conceptual framework and its updated information about world power relationships relevant to current American policy issues. It stands on its own intellectual foundation, and readers do not need to refer to earlier versions. Its special usefulness for students of international relations as well as for thoughtful citizens derives from its thorough integration of the main factors of power as perceived in the way that they influence strategic decisions.

In my experience, first as a government research analyst for thirty years and subsequently as a teacher in the School of Foreign Service at Georgetown University, I have encountered many specialists skilled in amassing detailed knowledge in a variety of fields but few generalists working to construct a comprehensive overview of the complex issues that confront national political leaders in actual life. My aim is to bridge the gulf separating the different research disciplines and provide a way of thinking systematically about power in the pragmatic fashion real decision makers are in practice obliged to do. My own conclusions on what this method indicates about U.S. defense and foreign policy planning are set forth in Part Three of this volume as a strategic blueprint for the 1980s.

PART I

Concept and Methodology

CHAPTER ONE

Politectonics: Measuring the Strength of Nations

The political and economic structure of international relations has never been more complex than in the last two decades of the twentieth century. Whatever the United States does or refrains from doing abroad materially affects the fate of nations and peoples whose welfare is tied to the fortunes of the strongest country in the world. The question uppermost in most foreign capitals is whether the economy, the military strength, and, in particular, coherence of purpose in the United States are adequate to the challenges ahead. The 1980s present great opportunities but also great dangers for the 20 percent of the peoples on the earth who belong to the Free World as distinct from the realm of Communist one-party dictatorships.

From the vantage point of Washington at the end of the 1970s it appears that the buoyancy and vigor of the U.S. behavior in earlier decades have trailed off into national uncertainty, indecisiveness, and self-doubt. Public confidence in governmental policymaking at the threshold of the 1980s is at its lowest point since before World War II. Americans have not fully recovered from the twin tragedies of the Watergate political disgrace and defeat in Vietnam. Allies of the United States show little trust in American leadership and security guarantees.

We all have to ask ourselves: What is happening in the international arena and the countries in it that has brought about this change, and just where does the United States really stand in the world balance of power? The answer lies in the strength of nations and the clusters of allied nations in terms of global geography, economic interdependence, military capability, and shifting political alignments.

A calculus of the critical elements of power as it is perceived and used in international politics is the only basis for assessing the gradual shift in the balance of power in recent decades among sovereign states. To determine where the United States stands strategically, particularly vis-à-vis the USSR, it is necessary to measure the strength of nations by some systematic method. To describe the fundamentally geographic but also essentially political methodology used in my strategic analysis, I have adopted a new word, "politectonics," i.e., political structuring. By this I denote the formation and breakup of international power groupings, mainly regional, but also shaped by cultural, political, economic, and military forces that determine the real balance in today's give-and-take relations among nations. Perhaps "geopolitical-tectonics" would be more accurate, but to go beyond five syllables in a deliberate coinage of a new word is more risky than I dare to be.

There is nothing very new in this approach, despite the new term. It labels a simple formula based on old truths. It is really a signal of a return to basics and the long perspective of historical change as a key to international relations. Shortly after the turn of the twentieth century, in 1904, the great British geographer Sir Halford Mackinder wrote an essay entitled "The Geographical Pivot of History" emphasizing the pivotal significance of political control of the human and material resources of the central Eurasian landmass. This emphasis increased as his ideas evolved more precisely down into the period of World War II. As the core of his thinking, Mackinder articulated a crucial concept in international relations by declaring that command of the Eurasian heartland (essentially central Europe and Russia, from the Urals to the Rhine) would lead to command, first of all of Eurasia, by far the largest of the continental landmasses, and eventually to domination of all the world's resources and peoples. This dictum is based on the fact that Eurasia and land-linked Africa, what Mackinder calls the "world island," comprises two-thirds of the land surface of the globe. He saw a fundamental difference between the land powers of the world island and the insular nations, such as the United States. He feared a day when Eurasia and land-linked Africa might become a united base of sea power, capable of outbuilding and outmanning the insular bases. The pros and cons of this concept have shaped the core of informed discussion of geopolitical theory ever since.

In part the concept is based on the American view of Alfred Thayer Mahan, who noted that North America, indeed the whole Western Hemisphere, is an island amid the world's oceans, and that sea power protecting transoceanic commerce has always been a key ingredient of the prosperity and influence of nations on the periphery of Eurasia or, as in the case of the United States, across the seas.[1] The special strategic problems of seafaring countries as compared with the land powers of central Europe and Asia added import to Mackinder's ideas about history and the future of international life. Napoleon, Hitler, and Stalin all came very close to seizing control of the heartland of Eurasia; all showed an interest in the Mideast and Africa, parts of the "world island." The Soviet Union commands most of the heartland region today. Mackinder and Mahan look more prescient all the time as we search for insights into present international circumstances and conflicts.

There is a striking analogy between political and strategic trends, on the one hand, and the terminology of new scholarly findings in the field of geology, on the other. It now seems that the earth's surface is made up of a number of separate "tectonic plates"[2] containing entire continents and immense stretches of the surrounding seabeds and oceans. There is a North American plate, a South American plate, a Pacific plate, a China plate, a Eurasian plate, an African plate, and an Indian Ocean–Australian plate as well as some smaller regional pieces of the earth's outer crustal shell.

These continental plates float on a more fluid inner core, and they have very slowly drifted back and forth over the millennia. Where they meet or pull apart, mountain ranges are thrust up, volcanic and seismic pressures erupt, great oceanic ridges and rifts are formed, and some underwater terrain slips beneath the edge of adjoining tectonic plates and is slowly ground back into the molten core of the earth.

A more graphic picture of what is taking place in a much quicker time frame in the shifting of international power in this century could hardly be found. The strength of nations and of the clusters of nations allied to one another waxes and wanes in conformity with rhythms of economic, military, and political changes, producing either growth and stability or conflict, erosion, and destruction.

No good word is in common use to describe the process of analyzing such structural international changes. The old term, "geopolitics," which derives from Mackinder's model for world trends, fell into disrepute largely as a result of distortions introduced in Germany by Karl Haushofer in Hitler's time, and also because of its tendency to emphasize only the relatively static and unchanging geographical relationships. In its place we now most often hear theorists talk of geometric patterns of power – triangular, pentagonal, etc. – among nations implicitly assumed to be as similar in interests and behavior as the countries of the nineteenth century "concert of Europe." The analogy is not very helpful in explaining the relations between open societies like the United States and the autarchic dictatorships of the Soviet Union or the People's Republic of China (PRC). The structure of international ties and conflicts is based on politics, geography, and economics, but not on any neat pattern of geometry. It is politectonics.

National Power in International Conflicts

In the rhetorical atmosphere of the United Nations all of the 162[3] more or less sovereign nations of the world are equal, but everyone is aware that in the real world some nations are much "more equal" than others. Some have tremendous power, others very little. In modern times the nation-state is the main aggregative unit of political force in international affairs.

A nation is a group of people, usually living in a specific territory, who share a common sense of history, customs, and (often) language. A state is nominally a sovereign body politic, although in practice the degree of sovereignty obviously varies. Many modern states are homogeneous nations and many nations are sovereign states. On the other hand, there are many states that are multinational.

In the USSR the dominant Great Russian population constitutes barely more than half of a country that includes many still quite distinct cultural minorities, concentrated in specific regions like the Ukraine or Kazakhstan, that by any normal definition would make up nations in their own right. The United States is a quite different type of nation-state with an astonishing mix of ethnic groups, many of whom deliberately came to North America to belong to a pluralistic body politic of remarkable political, cultural, and linguistic homogeneity.

Within national boundaries in many parts of the world, especially in Asia and Africa, tribalism or ethnic subnational loyalties are strong. Religious minorities and ethnic or linguistic factions battle in Ireland, Belgium, and India, and create agonizing tensions in Cyprus, South Africa, and even in Canada. The melting pot does not always really meld, not even in the United States, as fast or as thoroughly as once supposed. Nevertheless, the nation-state is the decisive political unit of action and responsibility in our era.

From the town meeting to the nation-state, communities of all types and sizes dispense power and privileges insofar as they act as a group. All of them must work out systems for sharing benefits and burdens, as well as for settling disputes among their members. They must also set up some kind of sanctions to enforce compliance with those settlements, sanctions vested in some constituted authority. The authority may be an absolute monarch with his army or a judiciary backed by civil police. Making decisions on all these matters is the business of the political leadership in office at any given time.

At this period of history, there is no single legitimately constituted power for the effective settlement of disagreements about global economic, military, and political conflicts. More important, there is no procedure in international relations which guarantees that sanctions will be applied to enforce compliance with such international settlements as can be agreed upon. The extent to which one country can pursue its international and domestic aims without regard to, or even against, the interests of others, is based in the final analysis on its own national power as compared with that of other nations. Power in the international arena can thus be defined simply as the ability of the government of one state to cause the government of another state to do something which the latter otherwise would not choose to do, or to cause the government of another state to refrain from doing something it wants to do, whether by persuasion, coercion, or outright military force.

Power is a subjective fact; it need not actually be brought into use to arrive at the results desired by those who wield it. A nation's leaders make decisions affecting foreign policy on the basis of projections of what they perceive their own power to be or of what they think is the power of others. Such projections may not always be accurate; a marked lag often exists between changing facts and perceptions of them, but the perceptions nonetheless determine governmental decisions.

International conflicts of interests, whether political, economic, or military, are played out like games of chess. Perceived power is a decisive factor, even if it only prevents another's action, as a chessman threatens every square on the board to which an opponent's piece might move. On an international chessboard the pattern of potential power and counter-power in the minds of the antagonists determines how the game proceeds from move to move and how it will end. Sometimes one nation carries out its aims to complete victory. More often the match is indecisive or flatly stalemated. Superfically nothing may appear to have happened. Only in desperate cases does the struggle move into a true end game, when – in international affairs – other levels of political and economic conflict are transcended and nations at last resort to war.

A study of national power, in the final analysis, is a study of the capacity to wage war, but it is also in the normal run of cases an appraisal of many other kinds of international competition or conflict, where differences are resolved within a political or an economic context. It is important to calculate carefully the capabilities and intentions of enemies or potential enemies, as well as those of allies and potential allies. A given country, seeking to maintain a favorable strategic balance in the world, needs to identify the countries sympathetic to its goals and strong enough to be helpful. It is at this point that moral and political considerations come into play in foreign policy and strategy.

A nation cannot afford to become mesmerized by the power potential of an adversary. An obsessive preoccupation with hostile governments can lead to error, either through exaggerated fear of the dangers they present or through anxiety to placate them. The sine qua non is to identify national objectives and to estimate whether or not they can be achieved. This will depend upon a nation's individual power, plus the power committed to its side by dependable alliances. Whether such alliances are voluntary or forced, they represent an important aspect and at times a limitation of national power.

For the first time in history two nations greater in most respects than any of the rest, the United States and the Soviet Union, plainly possess the capability of destroying with nuclear weapons the cities and total industrial structure of each other or of any nation. This fact acts as a restraint on the use of military force by all nations to pursue their national objectives at the expense of others. It also constitutes heavy psychological pressure on weaker nations to conform with the wishes of the two great nuclear powers and, in some cases, acts to prevent conflicts at levels of intensity lower than total warfare. In many cases, however, these restraints on resorting to small-scale military action or to revolutionary acts of violence and terror are diminishing because of the widespread belief that the two great adversary nuclear powers will never dare to use their immensely destructive weapons. For several years ahead in 1980s there will be a rough parity of U.S. and Soviet strategic nuclear forces, although the Soviet Union gains considerable psychological benefits in conflicts of lower intensity than war because it has a more dynamic nuclear arms building program.

Gradually, over the past quarter century, it has become apparent that maximum nuclear destruction is too awful – in the true sense of that much abused word – to contemplate. Thus, nuclear strikes are unlikely except as a desperate defensive last resort where such drastic punishment would fit the provocation. Beneath the umbrella of nuclear deterrence, however, nation-states or nonstate revolutionary groups are gaining substantial freedom to maneuver in committing lesser crimes, and they have to be restrained by the conventional methods of diplomacy, economic suasion, and the implicit threat of nonnuclear military force. In these circumstances it is imperative to try to measure the more intangible forms of national power as well as the various kinds of military strength in order to see where the balance of power lies and which way it is perceived to be shifting. Last-resort use of nuclear capability is a psychological factor of great effect in perceptions of strengths. However, it is only one of the several elements of national power viewed as instruments of policy, and it is usually not the decisive factor in a world where lower intensity conflicts are endemic.

The World Divided into Eleven Zones

Seeking a more realistic model for analyzing the power distribution among nations, I describe the world as composed of a number of discrete zones, whose relations are affected by both the relatively static factors of geography and the more fluid political, economic, and military factors of today's world. The future international alignments of major nations within these zones are crucial. As the map on the endpapers shows, there are eleven such zones, of which the primary ones are: (I) North and Central America, the heartland of which is the United States; (II) the USSR, the heartland of Eurasia; and (III) the PRC and the Asian Communist regimes in North Korea and Indochina that together occupy most of the mainland of East Asia.

On the periphery of Eurasia are five great peninsular or insular zones, the rimlands, that can be dominated from the center of the continental landmass but that also at this time are closely connected by transoceanic ties to other parts of the world, especially to the United States. These five are: (IV) West Europe, the crucial, long-disputed area stetching from Greece to the United Kingdom, an extended Eurasian peninsula from the viewpoint of the Soviet heartland; (V) the Mideast, a long belt of nations reaching from Iran across Asia Minor and the Arabian peninsula to the Arab littoral of North Africa; (VI) South Asia, the subcontinent; (VII) Southeast Asia beyond Indochina, the vast ocean archipelago area containing Indonesia, the Philippines, Singapore, Malaysia, Thailand, and Burma; and (VIII) Northeast Asia, the Japan–South Korea–China/Taiwan triangle.

These zones, the rimlands of Eurasia, are surrounded by an outer circle of continents and peoples. This circle comprises mainly the lands of the Southern Hemisphere, which group themselves in three zones: (IX) South America; (X) Central and Southern Africa; and (XI) Australia and New Zealand.

Needless to say, other dividing lines between zones could be picked out, and there are several geographical regions, like the Caribbean or the Arabian and Iranian geological entities, that could be viewed as separate politectonic subzones. The eleven basic zones, however, provide a useful structural overview of international relations today. The power of the individual nations in each zone and their links with one another, as well as their relationships with other zones, are the stuff with which world strategy and diplomacy deal. The slow, sometimes nearly imperceptible, shifting and drifting of the dominant national elements within or between clusters of politically allied nations, whether they are tightly controlled empires or voluntary associations of countries, constitute the phenomena we are observing and trying to measure.

The insights gained through this politectonic approach to international power largely coincide with the conventional wisdom concerning international power and conflict in recent years. Attempts to measure the power of nations individually or in groups are exceedingly difficult and inexact, whatever approach is used. Judging the trend in power relationships is even more difficult. A systematic effort along these lines may, however, clarify an understanding of the dangers and opportunities in the world around us in an era of fluidity, of strategic drift.

The 162 nations of the world are scattered rather unevenly among the eleven politectonic zones identified in the global maps on the following pages.

Elements of Power: The Formula

Obviously, a sound strategy for any nation requires an evaluation of national power and clusters of power in the international arena. This calculus must include an analysis of nuclear weaponry and its potential for the deterrence of war, but other elements of strength constitute crucial factors. Nonnuclear arms and forces, economic capacity, and economic resources materially affect the way national power is perceived and hence its effect. Coherence in formulating concepts of national purpose and the degree of consensus expressed as political will substantially alter the way military and economic power can be used.

National power, realistically described, is a mix of strategic, military, economic, and political strengths and weaknesses. It is determined in part by the military forces and the military establishment of a country but even more by the size and location of territory, the nature of frontiers, the populations, the raw-material resources, the economic structure, the technological development, the financial strength, the ethnic mix, the social cohesiveness, the stability of political processes and decision making, and finally, the intangible quality usually described as national spirit.

To ease the task of describing elements of international power in their various combinations, I have evolved a formula relating these factors. It is not a magic measuring rod, for many of the variables are not truly quantifiable. It merely

Zone I

Bahamas
Barbados
Canada
Costa Rica
Dominica
Dominican Republic
El Salvador
Grenada
Guatemala
Haiti
Honduras
Jamaica
Mexico
Nicaragua
Panama
Trinidad and Tobago
United States

Zone II

Bulgaria
Cuba
Czechoslovakia
Germany (GDR)
Hungary
Mongolia
Poland
Rumania
USSR

18

Zone III

China (PRC)
Kampuchea (Cambodia)
Korea, North
Laos
Vietnam

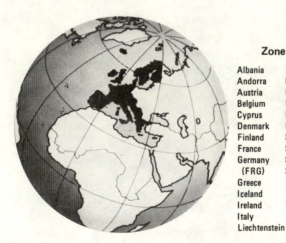

Zone IV

Albania	Luxembourg
Andorra	Malta
Austria	Monaco
Belgium	Netherlands
Cyprus	Norway
Denmark	Portugal
Finland	San Marino
France	Spain
Germany	Sweden
(FRG)	Switzerland
Greece	United Kingdom
Iceland	Vatican City
Ireland	Yugoslavia
Italy	
Liechtenstein	

Zone V

Algeria	Morocco
Bahrain	Oman
Cape Verde	Qatar
Djibouti	Saudi Arabia
Egypt	Sudan
Iran	Syria
Iraq	Tunisia
Israel	Turkey
Jordan	United Arab
Kuwait	Emirates
Lebanon	Yemen (Aden)
Libya	Yemen (Sana)
Mali	
Mauritania	

Zone VI

Afghanistan
Bangladesh
Bhutan
India
Maldives
Nepal
Pakistan
Sri Lanka

20

Zone VII

Burma
Indonesia
Malaysia
Philippines
Singapore
Thailand

Zone VIII

China/Taiwan
Japan
Korea, South

Zone IX

Argentina
Bolivia
Brazil
Chile
Colombia
Ecuador
Guyana
Paraguay
Peru
Surinam
Uruguay
Venezuela

Zone X

Angola	Malawi
Benin	Mauritius
Botswana	Mozambique
Burundi	Niger
Cameroon	Nigeria
Central African	Rwanda
Empire	Sao Tome and
Chad	Principe
Comoros	Senegal
Congo	Seychelles
Equatorial Guinea	Sierra Leone
Ethiopia	Somalia
Gabon	South Africa
Gambia	Swaziland
Ghana	Tanzania
Guinea	Togo
Guinea Bissau	Uganda
Ivory Coast	Upper Volta
Kenya	Zaire
Lesotho	Zambia
Liberia	Zimbabwe Rhodesia
Madagascar	

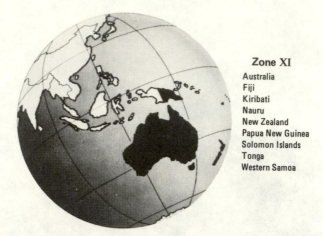

Zone XI

Australia
Fiji
Kiribati
Nauru
New Zealand
Papua New Guinea
Solomon Islands
Tonga
Western Samoa

provides a shorthand notation or index system to replace words and judgments. It is simply a systematic way to think about world power.

The formula is as follows:

$$P_p \;=\; (C + E + M) \times (S + W)$$

Its terms are defined thus:

P_p = perceived power
C = critical mass: population + territory
E = economic capability
M = military capability
S = strategic purpose
W = will to pursue national strategy

All of these terms will become clearer in the process of manipulating this formula to measure power as it is usually perceived in the international arena.

It only takes a careful look at the size and state of the economic development of the nations of the world to realize that the majority of them have relatively little impact on international affairs or even on important developments in their own regions. In a serious strategic assessment, perhaps only one-third of the nations have sufficient power to influence the pattern of the world balance of power at any one time. The rest either weigh so little in realistic power terms that they can be disregarded, or perhaps viewed as the political equivalent of iron filings, automatically arranging themselves around magnetic fields of force in the geographic zones or alliance systems to which they belong.

This is not to say the people of the less powerful countries are unimportant or that long-range strategic and humanitarian concerns can be ignored, especially since these also motivate citizens and governments. Yet, by any consistent standards of gross measurement, the preponderance of power appears to be in the hands of a relatively few nations.

Actually, some very simple quantifications appear to be adequate for the rough approximations of strength in world affairs on which most generalizations about the balance of power rest. We are dealing here in macrometrics, the technique of measuring power in a broad context of perception where precise detail is not very significant. The patterns and trends in international relationships are what we want to see—not the details.

In the same vein, while index numbers are used to weight values and quantify strengths, they reflect subjective and, in a sense, arbitrary judgments. They are used to convey easily and manipulate arithmetically estimates of comparative strengths and weaknesses among nations and groups of nations. It is crucial in using this calculus to understand that we are talking about perceptions of power by governments, which are often influenced by popular perceptions, and not necessarily about concrete elements of usable power. Power capable of being used seldom changes rapidly, but perceptions of it may vary, particularly in societies where public opinion is important and ideas circulate freely. Many of the judgments in this volume may need to be changed substantially as situations change. The macrometric values assigned in the following pages generally fit and also reflect the conventional perceptions of world power as it is commonly viewed at the beginning of the 1980s.

CHAPTER TWO

Polarity: Political and Geographic

By the opening of the twentieth century there were no new landward and seaward frontiers to explore. All continents had been discovered and, with the exception of frozen Antarctica, settled. The oceans had been traversed and regular sea-lanes across them established. Speed of travel and communication, ever on the increase, forced nations, large and small, to become more and more involved in each other's business. Most of them are by now quite interdependent. Their search for prosperity, influence, and security had to take place within the community of established modern states, each with its own ideology, its own aims and ambitions.

A nation's status in the world community and its success in achieving its aims and ambitions depend upon the simple verities of geography, economics, and politics. However, the strictly geographic substructure of where a nation stands in international relationships is in many cases substantially modified by political and economic affinities and incompatibilities. Political traditions become cherished parts of national culture; among traditional cultures like calls to like and alien ideas are in general looked at askance. Trade ties that mutually benefit and enrich the lives of the people within bilateral or multilateral commercial systems are powerful forces pulling in the direction of cooperation. Conversely, compe-

25

tition for scarce raw materials or markets can breed bitter international enmities.

The Horseshoe Spectrum

These complex economic and political factors taken together in a broad context reveal that there is in the twentieth century a kind of polarity based on fundamental societal differences. Most modern nations can be classified somewhere along the spread of a novel but rather simple political horseshoe spectrum (Graphic I) reflecting major present-day tendencies, and when they are so arranged two clusters of associated nations appear at opposite sides of the horseshoe figure that best fits the facts of national types.

In laying out this spectrum, to avoid ethnocentrism or pejorative terms I have deliberately avoided the conventional straight line classification based on left-right or conservative-liberal distinctions.

LEFT	CENTER	RIGHT
Revolutionary Radical	Liberal Conservative	Reactionary

These labels confuse, more often than clarify, today's political behavior groupings.

The present Communist states of the Soviet Union and the People's Republic of China fall into place as state-owned economies on the left polar end of the spectrum. On the right polar end the powerful Fascist dictatorships of our era in Germany and Italy conformed to the category of corporate states, very similar in political philosophy and style. They disappeared, perhaps not forever, during World War II.

There is no very good word to describe these new-style dictatorships, but totalitarian is the most often used because it suggests the absolute, comprehensive character of the political control they seek. The models of such totalitarianism—Stalin's USSR, Mao Tse-tung's PRC, Hitler's Germany,

GRAPHIC I

The Political Horseshoe Spectrum

PLURALISM

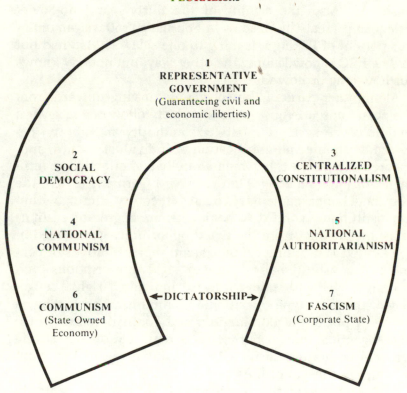

1
REPRESENTATIVE
GOVERNMENT
(Guaranteeing civil and
economic liberties)

2
SOCIAL
DEMOCRACY

3
CENTRALIZED
CONSTITUTIONALISM

4
NATIONAL
COMMUNISM

5
NATIONAL
AUTHORITARIANISM

6
COMMUNISM
(State Owned
Economy)

←DICTATORSHIP→

7
FASCISM
(Corporate State)

TOTALITARIANISM

and Mussolini's Italy – exhibit something new in their control techniques and something very old in their despotic forms of politics. Calling them dictatorships of the left or right is rather irrelevant. In keeping with conventional left-right classifications they are separated by the open gap in the horseshoe figure, but in fact their political morals and methods are so similar that they can cooperate across the open end when strategy demands it, as the Hitler-Stalin pact of 1939 demonstrated. Also, the signing of the thirty-year Sino-Soviet Friendship Treaty in Moscow in February 1950 was an ominous portent of Peking's "leaning to one side," as Mao had put it. The PRC is now leaning the other way, but nobody knows for how long or how far.

Along other parts of the spectrum, curving upward from the polar ends, are those societies which follow one of several middle courses, steering between authority and liberty, between discipline and gratification of individual wishes, and, theoretically at least, between anarchy and effective government. Examples among them are: West Germany (FRG), the best model of parliamentary social democracy, aiming within a constitutional context to achieve some degree of egalitarianism as distinct from the equal opportunity guaranteed in the United States; France and Japan, representatives of centralized constitutionalism under rigid prescriptions and restraints, yet with safeguards for individual rights; Yugoslavia, the archetype of national communism, struggling to be free from Soviet domination; and South Korea or Brazil and Argentina, the most obvious current exemplars of strong national authoritarianism with substantial regard for maintaining the consent of the governed.

At the center of the spectrum, at the top and centrally located between the two polar ends, is the group of societies that follow the pluralistic model of representative government, either parliamentary or presidential-congressional. The modern nation-states, in their five hundred years or so of evolution, have experimented with numerous political ways of providing the benefits of social discipline without sacrificing the rights of individuals to pursue their happiness.

The British evolved the system of resolving conflicts and

sharing burdens and benefits through compromises arrived at in a representative parliament—by ballot rather than on the battlefield. The United States developed a variant with the separation of powers between executive and legislative authority. The American Bill of Rights defines the core of liberties that individuals and minorities are guaranteed in this kind of society, most accurately described as pluralism. The emphasis is on toleration of diverse groups with different aims so long as they do not damage the common aims of the majority. Energy and initiatives originate among the citizens, with government acting somewhat as an umpire and sponsor of compromises likely to create a plurality in its support.

Pluralism is the opposite of totalitarianism, where government forces goals and standards of behavior downward on individuals and majority groups to conform with the decisions at the top. A final important distinction is that a pluralistic society includes among the rights of citizens the freedom to satisfy consumers' economic wants through private enterprise for private profit. This form of economic activity, with initiative coming from the bottom up, where it can be regulated if necessary, rather than from the top down, has always tended to lead to a private or corporate search for materials and markets outside national boundaries. Hence both the British and U.S. economies have stressed comparatively free international trade as well as protection of economic and political freedoms at home.

The United States and the major countries of West Europe, from which the largest part of the original U.S. population and cultural tradition stems, provide the most successful models for the kind of government that has clear limits on arbitrary rule, careful safeguards for election of representative leaders, and legal protection for the right of minorities to exist safely together within the confines of a pluralistic state. Civil liberties, human rights, electoral privileges, representative government, and equality of economic opportunity are the hallmarks of these nations which, somewhat inexactly, label themselves democratic, whether they are in fact social democracies, parliamentary systems, or presidential-congressional governments. The label "democratic" itself has become almost meaningless since it has been cynically appropriated and used by the Communist dictatorships. Pluralism connotes tolerance of diverse elements in the body politic of nations. Rather than constraining policy to follow a fixed ideological goal, it allows for shifting majorities to form a consensus, from time to time, for pragmatic purposes.

Recently fewer rather than more countries are trying to follow the British–U.S. model of government. The classification of states is full of ambiguity, but it is probably valid as a broad generalization to say that only 20 percent of the approximately 4.3 billion people in the world live in these kinds of relatively free, pluralistic national societies. About 45 percent of the world population are in an in-between status—not free, not strictly totalitarian. The range is from noncommunist, often rather ineffective, authoritarian governments to almost free but imperfect representative governments of various kinds. Some are breaking down into near anarchy of the libertarian or egalitarian type usually called left, and some avoid anarchy by turning to arbitrary authoritarianism, that is, to the right.[4] This leaves about 35 percent of the world population in states with one-party absolute dictatorships, closed societies, and autarkic command economies.

Since the two strongest positions on the horseshoe spectrum are those occupied by pluralist or representative governments at the center and those held by dictatorships at the two polar ends, the world is essentially bipolar. The forms of government between these two positions tend to meld either up or down, favoring alignment ideologically and politically with either of the dominant forms of society.

Much has been written in recent years about the passage of world affairs from an era of bipolarity to a condition of multipolarity. There is some truth in these assertions. Nations cluster together in groups such as those formed of the oil rich, the industrially advanced, the economically disadvantaged. In many respects, however, the emphasis on multipolarity is dangerously wrong. The world is still, to a remarkable extent, divided between a sphere of influence dominated by the USSR, and a much less clearly delimited sphere of influence dominated—less firmly—by the United States. There are some exceptions to this neat bipolar division, and the PRC is perhaps the only one due consideration. Mainland China rightfully belongs to the USSR sphere of influence, yet in the post-Mao era the Chinese have flirted off and on with the United States, especially when they felt vulnerable to Soviet pressure. For all practical purposes, therefore, the international power structure is centered in Moscow and Washington, despite the proliferation of smaller nations and the increase in strength of some of the secondary powers.

Strategic Bipolarity

The best way to examine the strategic location and the interrelationships of nations is to study a globe – not a flattened Mercator map projection of it – looking directly at the North Pole. Next best is to study the polar map projection on the endpapers of this book. It shows how the USSR and the United States confront each other across the northern Arctic wastes. Most of the continental landmasses surround the North Pole, and most of the earth's surface in the Southern Hemisphere is water. The great multicontinent Eurasia, including the USSR and the PRC, lies totally within the Northern Hemisphere, as does the North American continent, directly opposite it. The United States is centrally positioned between Canada and Mexico. With the Caribbean countries, they constitute a single strategic entity stretching from the North Pole to the Panama Canal.

In this strictly geographic sense, whether or not it likes the situation, Canada becomes an important extension of the northern U.S. strategic border. Thus the geography of Canada impels its identification with North American security quite apart from the multiple economic and political ties between Canada and the United States, and indeed apart from the occasional frictions that arise between Washington and Ottawa. The Caribbean islands, Mexico, and Central America are strategically linked with the United States and with continental defense perimeters. This remains true even though these areas are also drawn culturally and politically toward

South America and other regions (i.e., Britain, Spain, or France) and in some instances flaunt an anti-Yankee attitude on international issues.

Putting it crudely and literally, everything else in international affairs is peripheral; not unimportant but marginal to matters of primary strategic concern to the USSR and the United States. Other nations cluster in areas abutting on Soviet territory around the edges of the vast Eurasian continent; many nations are linked by sea-lanes to one another and to North America; some nations, of course, are pulled in both directions at once, and a few try to escape their natural geographic linkages. Thus we see Castro's Cuba anomalously linked to Moscow, while moves in Angola, Ethiopia, and Zambia in Africa and Afghanistan and Yemen (Aden) in the Mideast are designed to create new cross-regional politectonic links.

This basic geographic and strategic polarity of North America and the Soviet heartland of Eurasia has long been apparent, but the nuclear missile age for the first time added enormous significance to the polar factor because it leaves the two continental superpowers locked in position just thirty minutes away from each other's military capability to destroy all the cities and most of the people in both countries. This power potential will probably never be used by either of the two deadly scorpions in the bottle as long as the strategic nuclear power remains balanced, but all other international relationships are profoundly altered by it. The bipolar relationship between the United States and the USSR, both of which tend to dominate the regions of the earth in which they lie, is crucial to all international developments.

The clustering of various nations around the Soviet Union and the United States is the dominating strategic feature of the international landscape of the second half of the twentieth century.

PART II

Assessment of the Power of Nations

CHAPTER THREE

Critical Mass: Population and Territory
$$P_p = (C + E + M) \times (S + W)$$

The first factor in the formula for measuring perceived power in international affairs is what I have called "*C*" or "critical mass," a judgment on the size or mass of a nation. This perception is often blurred or diffuse, but it is fundamentally based on the amount of territory under a state's control and the number of people supported economically by that territory. While it is hard to quantify, there does seem to be a kind of critical mass—a reflection of population and area—that a nation must ordinarily possess to make itself felt in world affairs.

In view of this age-old fact, we begin our measurement effort with this oversimplification: $P_p = C$. Obviously, additional factors and coefficients are needed for a more accurate formula of perceived power. It is revealing, nevertheless, to make a first approximation of the strength of nations in the international balance in this traditional way.

Population

The first factor to look at in considering the importance of states is population. It is the sense of community among human beings that identifies the nation-state and infuses it with life. People exploit the raw economic resources of the territory they live in and develop the political and social traditions that shape national cultures. The spirit and competence of the individual human beings in a society, in the long run, may count as much as or more than the concrete and material resources a nation possesses. Population size is clearly a major element in international perceptions of whether or not a country constitutes a critical mass in terms of national power. Table 1 ranks all of the 162 nations, placing those with the largest populations at the top and descending to the smallest.

There are roughly 4.3 billion people in the world. The sixteen nations with populations of over 50 million include most of the countries commonly perceived as world powers. Among them are the People's Republic of China, India, the USSR, the United States, the United Kingdom, Italy, and France. The international community always pays some heed to the policies and fortunes of these countries. It is true that nations with a population of 15 to 50 million also constitute a force to be reckoned with when others think of trying to influence or coerce them. Twenty-seven nations have populations in this range. Altogether these forty-three most populated states have within their borders more than 3.8 billion, or nearly 90 percent, of the world's inhabitants. In fact, approximately one-half of the entire global population resides in the PRC, India, the USSR, and the United States.

It is hard in normal cases to think of nations with a population of less than 15 million as having truly great power in their own right, independent of the interests or actions of larger nations. There are eighty-one countries in this size range. A few—for example, Saudi Arabia (8 million), Israel (3.7 million), New Zealand (3.2 million), and Singapore (2.3 million)—have a disproportionate influence in international affairs because of some special circumstance, such as advantageous strategic location. The thirty-eight smallest nations have populations of less than one million, and their influence, if any, is based on other qualities. The very smallest entity, the Vatican City, has an enormous spiritual impact through the Papacy.

Table 1. Population, 1978[5]

Country	Population (millions)	Perceived Power Weights
The 43 Largest Countries (population 15 million or more)		
1. China (PRC)*	1,014	25
2. India*	668	25
3. USSR	262	50
4. United States	219	50
5. Indonesia	146	36
6. Brazil	123	30
7. Japan	115	29
8. Bangladesh	87	22
9. Pakistan	79	20
10. Nigeria	69	17
11. Mexico	67	17
12. Germany (FRG)	61	15
13. Italy	57	14
14. United Kingdom	56	14
15. France	53	13
16. Vietnam	52	13
17. Thailand	46	12
18. Philippines	46	12
19. Turkey	44	11
20. Egypt	40	10
21. Korea, South	39	10
22. Spain	38	10
23. Iran	36	9
24. Poland	35	9
25. Burma	33	8
26. Ethiopia	31	8
27. South Africa	27	7
28. Zaire	27	7
29. Argentina	26	6
30. Colombia	26	6
31. Canada	23	6
32. Yugoslavia	22	5
33. Rumania	22	5
34. Morocco	19	5
35. Korea, North	18	5
36. Algeria	18	5
37. Sudan	18	5
38. China/Taiwan	17	4
39. Peru	17	4
40. Tanzania	17	4
41. Germany (GDR)	16	4
42. Czechoslovakia	15	4
43. Kenya	15	4

Table 1. (Cont.)

Country	Population (millions)	Country	Population (millions)
Under 15 Million (no weights attached)			
Afghanistan	14.5	Malaysia	13.1
Venezuela	14.5	Uganda	13.0
Sri Lanka	14.4	Iraq	12.7
Australia	14.3	Ghana	11.5
Netherlands	14.0	Chile	10.8
Nepal	13.8	Hungary	10.8
Under 10 Million			
Mozambique	9.9	Upper Volta	6.6
Cuba	9.9	Angola	6.5
Belgium	9.8	Tunisia	6.3
Portugal	9.8	Mali	6.3
Greece	9.4	Switzerland	6.3
Bulgaria	8.9	Kampuchea (Cambodia)	6.0**
Sweden	8.3	Guinea	6.0
Syria	8.3	Malawi	5.8
Madagascar	8.2	Haiti	5.6
Cameroon	8.1	Zambia	5.5
Saudi Arabia	8.0	Dominican Republic	5.5
Ecuador	7.7	Senegal	5.4
Austria	7.5	Bolivia	5.1
Zimbabwe–Rhodesia	7.4	Denmark	5.1
Ivory Coast	7.4	Yemen (Sana)	5.1
Guatemala	6.7	Niger	5.1
Under 5 Million			
Finland	4.7	Albania	2.6
El Salvador	4.6	Lebanon	2.6
Rwanda	4.5	Togo	2.5
Chad	4.5	Nicaragua	2.4
Burundi	4.3	Singapore	2.3
Norway	4.1	Jamaica	2.2
Israel	3.7	Costa Rica	2.1
Laos	3.6	Central African Empire	1.9
Honduras	3.6	Panama	1.8
Somalia	3.4	Yemen (Aden)	1.8
Benin	3.3	Liberia	1.8
Sierra Leone	3.3	Mongolia	1.6
Ireland	3.2	Mauritania	1.6
New Zealand	3.2	Congo	1.5
Paraguay	3.1	Lesotho	1.3
Papua New Guinea	3.0	Bhutan	1.3

Table 1. (Cont.)

Country	Population (millions)	Country	Population (millions)
Jordan	3.0	Kuwait	1.2
Uruguay	2.9	Trinidad and Tobago	1.1
Libya	2.8		

Under 1 Million (population in thousands)

Country	Population	Country	Population
Mauritius	927	Bahamas	229
Guyana	818	Iceland	224
Botswana	760	Solomon Islands	215
United Arab Emirates	656†	Djibouti	180†
Cyprus	642	Qatar	165
Guinea-Bissau	625	Western Samoa	155
Fiji	615	Maldives	143
Gambia	576	Grenada	106
Gabon	575	Tonga	91
Oman	558	Sao Tome and Principe	82
Swaziland	533	Dominica	78
Surinam	388	Seychelles	64
Luxembourg	358	Kiribati	55
Equatorial Guinea	339	Andorra	29†
Malta	326†	Monaco	25†
Comoros	320	Liechtenstein	22
Cape Verde	318	San Marino	21†
Bahrain	289	Nauru	7†
Barbados	260	Vatican City	1†

Total Population	4,358 million

*These nations with very high populations and very low per capita GNP (over 500 million people and under U.S. $500 per capita GNP), at present and probably through the decade of the 1980s, are bound to suffer from the economic burden of large impoverished populations more than they benefit from the manpower. They are accordingly reduced in perceived power weight by an arbitrary 50 percent. Nevertheless, in common perceptions, such very large populations cause countries to be taken seriously by other nations. For example, the People's Republic of China, weak in most regards other than population, is treated as a great power almost universally simply because it would be an unthinkable burden to establish a military occupation over the entire country.

**No accurate information is available, but it is a moderate estimate to suppose that the population declined by about 2 million during the brutal period of the rule of the fanatic Communist, Pol Pot.

†Non-1978 populations: Malta (1977), Andorra (1976), Vatican City (1977), San Marino (1977), Djibouti (1972), Nauru (1969), United Arab Emirates (1975), Monaco (1976).

The USSR and the United States, with populations of 200 million, receive optimum perceived power ratings of 50. Weights of 25 are given to the two most populous nations, the People's Republic of China and India, whose inert, impoverished masses are a handicap rather than an advantage. Smaller nations are weighted downward to scale roughly in proportion to the size of their population. They are separated into clusters at arbitrary breakpoints in size of population selected purely for convenience of comparisons. The lowest rating noted in Table 1 is 4. Nations with populations under 15 million are not weighted in this ranklist despite the fact that a number of these smaller nations are accorded a good deal of respect internationally on the basis of characteristics other than population size.

Territory

Land area is also basic to our weighting system of critical mass. The distribution of territory among nations is as inequitable as the distribution of population. In general, although not in every case, large territory means ample raw material resources for people to exploit economically. The surface of the earth covers approximately 197 million square miles, and 71 percent, or 140 million square miles, is water. The rest, or 57.5 million square miles, is land; of this total area, 5.5 million square miles are in icebound Antarctica. Thus there are 52 million square miles of habitable land surface. The first six countries in size, the USSR, Canada, the PRC, the United States, Brazil, and Australia, are on a level by themselves, each occupying 3 million square miles of territory or more—in the case of the USSR considerably more. (See Table 2.) Seventeen "big boys"—each occupying more than one-half million square miles of territory—together cover a total of approximately 35 million square miles, more than two-thirds of the globe's inhabited land surface.

The three largest nations have enormous areas that are waste, desert, or are otherwise ill-suited for any kind of cultivation. Only about 26 percent of the Soviet Union's vast

Table 2. Territory[6]
(in thousands of square miles)

Country	Area	Perceived Power Weights
1. USSR	8,600	50
2. Canada	3,800	50
3. China (PRC)	3,700	50
4. United States	3,600	50
5. Brazil	3,300	50
6. Australia	3,000	50
7. India*	1,200	27
8. Argentina*	1,100	25
9. Sudan	967	13
10. Algeria	950	12
11. Zaire	905	12
12. Saudi Arabia	900	12
13. Mexico	764	10
14. Indonesia*	736	20
15. Libya	679	10
16. Iran	636	9
17. Mongolia	604	8
18. Chad	496	7
19. Peru	496	7
20. Niger	489	7
21. Angola	481	7
22. South Africa*	472	16
23. Mali	465	6
24. Ethiopia	455	6
25. Colombia	440	5
26. Bolivia	424	5
27. Mauritania	419	5
28. Egypt*	386	15
29. Tanzania	363	5
30. Nigeria	357	5
31. Venezuela	352	5
32. Pakistan	310	5
33. Mozambique	304	5
34. Turkey*	296	15
35. Zambia	288	5
36. Chile*	286	15
37. Burma	262	5
38. Afghanistan	250	5
39. Somalia*	246	15
40. Central African Empire	242	5
41. Madagascar	230	5
42. Kenya	225	5
43. Botswana	220	5
44. France*	213	15
45. Thailand	198	5
46. Spain*	195	15
47. Cameroon	184	5

Table 2. (Cont.)

Country	Area	Perceived Power Weights
48. Papua New Guinea	183	5
49. Sweden	173	5
50. Iraq	172	5
51. Morocco	158	5
52. Paraguay	157	5
53. Zimbabwe-Rhodesia	151	5
54. Japan*	143	15
55. Congo	135	5
56. Finland	130	5
57. Malaysia	128	5
58. Vietnam*	127	15
59. Norway*	125	15
60. Ivory Coast	125	5
61. Poland	121	5
62. Italy*	116	15
63. Philippines*	116	15
64. Yemen (Aden)*	111	15
65. Ecuador	106	5
66. Upper Volta	106	5
67. New Zealand*	104	15
68. Gabon	102	5
69. Yugoslavia	99	5
70. Germany (FRG)*	96	15
71. Guinea	95	5
72. United Kingdom*	94	15
73. Ghana	92	5
74. Rumania	92	5
75. Laos	91	5
76. Uganda	91	5
77. Guyana	83	5
78. Oman	82	5
79. Senegal	76	5
80. Yemen (Sana)	75	5
81. Uruguay	72	5
82. Syria	72	5
83. Kampuchea (Cambodia)	70	5
84. Tunisia	63	5
85. Nicaragua	57	5
86. Surinam	55	5
87. Bangladesh	55	5
88. Nepal	55	5
89. Greece	51	5

Table 2. (Cont.)

Countries Added Because of Location	Area	Perceived Power Weights
90. Iceland*	40	10
91. Korea, South*	38	10
92. Panama*	29	10
93. Denmark*	17	10
94. China/Taiwan*	14	10

*A bonus weight of ten points is added for these twenty-four nations occupying strategic locations on or near critical sea-lanes or ocean chokepoints and also being perceived as having some realistic near-term capability to exercise control of these locations. The last five states on the list occupy territory of less than 50,000 sq. mi. but are listed only because they are located at critically important strategic points on the globe. In the Persian Gulf–Red Sea–Indian Ocean area other countries that are strategically located now have insufficient power to exercise that control. Iran, for example, has just lost its capability as a result of internal insecurity, and other states like Iraq have not yet filled the vacuum. On the other hand, a small state, Yemen (Aden), virtually a Soviet puppet, does have the capability under Soviet protection to threaten shipping in the Red Sea and the Gulf of Aden.

territory is arable, cultivated, or natural pastureland, while most of the rest is permafrost. Canada has even less arable or cultivated land (6 percent), and the PRC little more (11 percent). This factor scales the territorial importance of these giants down considerably. Of the next three continental-sized nations, the highly developed United States still has nearly half (46 percent) of its territory in arable land or cultivated pasture. Australia and Brazil are relatively underdeveloped. Australia has 64 percent of its land cultivated or arable, while Brazil has only 17 percent. For ranklist purposes they are all given the maximum power weight, 50.

Not far behind, at another level of size, India and Argentina have almost half or more of their land cultivated or arable, and both are in strategic locations of considerable value. Therefore they get a bonus of 10 added to their perceived power weights. As a result they stand out at the head of the nations of less than 3 million square miles of territory.

The last nine of the "big boys," each occupying between one-half million and one million square miles of territory, have enormous desert areas within their boundaries. All of them except Saudi Arabia, Libya, and Mongolia are on the list of the forty-three most populous nations, reaching critical mass in the eyes of the world for this reason as well as for territorial size. If our territorial ranklist is extended further down to include all nations exceeding 50,000 square miles, the cutoff point would then be fixed to include eighty-nine nations. As explained in the note at the end of Table 2 an additional five states—China/Taiwan, South Korea, Denmark, Iceland, and Panama—are added because of their strategic locations.

Of the ninety-four states thus listed, many (fifty-four) have a population of less than 15 million, and some of them much less. A small population may mean the country is not likely to be developed into a modern, powerful nation, or at least that the prospect is in the distant future. Despite the desert character of most of the land and the small number of people of Saudi Arabia, and to a lesser extent Libya, the strategic and economic value of petroleum resources insures international power in keeping with the vastness of their territories. Each nation is a separate case, but perceptions tend to reflect the crude facts of territorial extent as one determining factor in establishing the critical mass of a country. Weights indicating perceived power are assigned roughly in proportion to the amount of territory each state possesses, with the truly large continental, or quasi-continental, nations heading the list at the maximum weight of 50.

Some nations, not so large, control particularly important land or sea corridors, such as the Suez Canal, the Bosporus, the Strait of Malacca, and the Iceland–United Kingdom chokepoint in the North Atlantic. Still others have achieved considerable impact because of control of valuable natural resources or by developing special economic skills or commodities which are in demand in international trade. A substantial bonus value (10 points) is added for those states occupying crucial strategic locations and having some power to exert control or denial of their use.

Leaving these special cases aside, a large area, if accompanied by a large population, almost automatically confers the status of power on a nation and will be so interpreted by strategists and makers of foreign policy. This image of power is what I call critical mass. The eight largest nations geographically have populations of over 15 million except for Australia; with only 14.3 million people, Australia is a marginal member of this top group, sustained in it by the impression of having vast natural resources to exploit as the population grows. In the southern reaches of both the Pacific and Indian oceans, Australia is the major power – flanked by a congenial smaller neighbor, New Zealand. These eight are perceived by any standard as nations of consequence. The remaining nations in the list of ninety-four are assigned power weights in descending order roughly proportional to the ratio of their territory compared with that of the United States. No country listed is given less than a weight of 5 because perceptions of this sort are generally rather imprecise, and middle-sized nations are often viewed as much alike in crude strategic calculations.

Perceived Power for Critical Mass

If we add the appropriate weights for the largest territorial holdings to the forty-three nations with the largest populations, we have a consolidated ranklist providing weights for the term C in the perceived power formula. All countries with territories of more than 500,000 square miles and populations of more than 15,000,000 are included in this ranklist of critical mass, Table 3.

There remain many refinements in the power equation still to be made for each country. On the basis of particular economic, military, and political factors, some nations must be designated as powerful in a special sense because of those factors even though both their population and territory are small; these factors will be calculated in later chapters. Thus, if countries later come into consideration because of other strengths, their total power rating will at that point also be increased on the basis of the weight values given them for territorial extent, even though the territorial factor alone is too

Table 3. Critical Mass Assessment,* 1978
(population and territory)

Country	Perceived Power Weights		
	Population	Territory	Total
1. USSR	50	50	100
2. United States	50	50	100
3. Brazil	30	50	80
4. China (PRC)	25	50	75
5. Indonesia**	36	20	56
6. Canada	6	50	56
7. India**	25	27	52
8. Australia	—	50	50
9. Japan**	29	15	44
10. Argentina**	6	25	31
11. Germany (FRG)**	15	15	30
12. United Kingdom**	14	15	29
13. Italy**	14	15	29
14. France**	13	15	28
15. Vietnam**	13	15	28
16. Mexico	17	10	27
17. Bangladesh	22	5	27
18. Philippines**	12	15	27
19. Turkey**	11	15	26
20. Egypt**	10	15	25
21. Spain**	10	15	25
22. Pakistan	20	5	25
23. South Africa**	7	16	23
24. Nigeria	17	5	22
25. Korea, South**	10	10	20
26. Zaire	7	12	19
27. Iran	9	9	18
28. Sudan	5	13	18
29. Thailand	12	5	17
30. Algeria	5	12	17
31. China/Taiwan**	4	10	14
32. Poland	9	5	14
33. Ethiopia	8	6	14
34. Burma	8	5	13
35. Saudi Arabia	—	12	12
36. Peru	4	7	11
37. Colombia	6	5	11
38. Yugoslavia	5	5	10
39. Libya	—	10	10
40. Morocco	5	5	10
41. Rumania	5	5	10
42. Kenya	4	5	9
43. Tanzania	4	5	9
44. Mongolia	—	8	8
45. Korea, North	5	—	5

Table 3. (Cont.)

| Country | Perceived Power Weights | | |
	Population	Territory	Total
46. Czechoslovakia	4	–	4
47. Germany (GDR)	4	–	4
		Total	1,292

*Includes all nations with populations of 15,000,000 or more and/or territory exceeding 500,000 square miles.

**Indicates the sixteen nations with a critical mass of population and/or territory which have, in addition, a bonus weight of 10 points for occupying territory located strategically on or near critical sea-lanes or ocean chokepoints. Some countries assigned bonus points for strategic location are not on this list because their population is less than 15,000,000 and their territory is less than 500,000 square miles.

small to qualify them for the consolidated list of critical mass at this point. This procedure generally gives a little more importance to people than to territory, since populous countries of an adequate size can exploit economic resources, mobilize armies, and bring their influence to bear on others. In other words, in some cases a large and industrious population can offset the disadvantage of a small territory.

To a limited degree, a large territory also can offset a small population. On this basis the ranklist includes four countries—Australia, Saudi Arabia, Libya, and Mongolia—solely because of their extensive territories. Three other countries—North Korea, Czechoslovakia, and Germany (GDR)—receive a place on the list solely because of their populations. In addition sixteen nations, marked with a double asterisk, gain bonus points in their territorial assessment as was indicated in Table 2 because they command strategic locations on or near important sea-lanes or ocean chokepoints.

Since an arbitrary scale of 100 has been adopted for maximum critical mass, it is clear that the USSR and the United States have an optimum size of population related to territorial base, and hence they are in a unique category that is widely perceived as the top level of power status. They are superpowers when weighted in the combined factor C of population and territory, as in many other respects. China, by its own admission, does not make the superpower grade, mainly because of overpopulation. India's population is also too large for its territorial resources, as indicated in Table 1. The consolidated ranklist compiled according to these judgments about perceived power weights totals forty-seven nations.

The forty-seven major countries in the world as calculated purely on the basis of population and possession of land are those that most observers of international events would normally call to mind. The big four are the USSR, the United States, Brazil, and China (PRC). These four are prima facie of consequence or certainly of so much potential consequence that any assessment of the international balance of power must pay special attention to them. This critical mass assessment needs much refinement but it conforms to most subjective judgments of conditions in the world today.

It may be useful now to note how these major nations are distributed among the politectonic zones of the globe. They provide the foundation, though not the exclusive subject, of our ongoing assessment. The weights assigned constitute units of perceived power, a kind of abstract measure that I am tempted to call "politectons" to emphasize that perceived power is not necessarily identical with actual power. In any case these units give a preliminary quantification of the international importance of the leading nations in each strategic zone and hence of the zones themselves in the eyes of the national political leaders and strategic planners in each country. (See Table 4.)

It is apparent that some zones are of great importance, owing to the critical mass of the nations in them, but are weakened by political separatism and fragmentation at the present time. Intraregional conflicts in the Mideast and in Central and Southern Africa are especially damaging to regional exercise of national power and hence to world perceptions of the importance of these zones. For example, Ethiopia is at present almost a captive — evidently a willing captive — of Soviet and Cuban military power. If this situation persists for

Table 4. Distribution of Perceived Power
by Politectonic Zones, 1978
(critical mass)

Politectonic Zone	Country	Perceived Power Weights	Zonal Total
I	United States	100	
	Canada	56	183
	Mexico	27	
II	USSR	100	
	Poland	14	
	Rumania	10	140
	Mongolia	8	
	Germany (GDR)	4	
	Czechoslovakia	4	
III	China (PRC)	75	
	Vietnam*	28	108
	Korea, North*	5	
IV	Germany (FRG)	30	
	United Kingdom	29	
	Italy	29	151
	France	28	
	Spain	25	
	Yugoslavia**	10	
V	Turkey	26	
	Egypt	25	
	Iran	18	
	Sudan	18	136
	Algeria	17	
	Saudi Arabia	12	
	Libya	10	
	Morocco	10	
VI	India	52	
	Bangladesh	27	104
	Pakistan	25	

Table 4. (Cont.)

Politectonic Zone	Country	Perceived Power Weights	Zonal Total
VII	Indonesia	56	113
	Philippines	27	
	Thailand	17	
	Burma	13	
VIII	Japan	44	78
	Korea, South	20	
	China/Taiwan	14	
IX	Brazil	80	133
	Argentina	31	
	Colombia	11	
	Peru	11	
X	South Africa	23	96
	Nigeria	22	
	Zaire	19	
	Ethiopia	14	
	Kenya	9	
	Tanzania	9	
XI	Australia	50	50
	Total for all zones (47 nations)		1,292

*Including Communist Vietnam and North Korea as part of Communist Asia is dubious politically and strategically, as distinct from geographically, but regional links have some importance despite the conflict between Communist states in the area. The lesser Communist countries, Kampuchea and Laos, not important enough to appear on this chart, illustrate vividly the dissarray of the Communist regimes in Southeast Asia.

**Including nonaligned Yugoslavia as part of West Europe is dubious strategically, as distinct from geographically. Without it, the value for West Europe would be 141, almost identical with the USSR and East Europe combined.

a little longer it ought to be listed along with Cuba as part of the Soviet politectonic zone. Another anomaly is South Africa, which geopolitically is the dynamic economic power in Southern Africa and a natural ally of the United States and West Europe; yet the hostility toward South Africa on the part of the black African states has virtually isolated it from constructive regional or international alliance relations.

The forty-seven nations arranged in their politectonic zones are in a general sense the principal eligible players in the game of international politics. Many of them are not yet able to take a strong, independent position and have not formed stable alliance relationships. A few others will emerge as eligible players because of economic or military strengths realized apart from size of population or territory. Our politectonic assessment is only at a first-phase plateau. More refined measurements must be introduced.

CHAPTER FOUR

Economic Capability
$$P_p = (C + E + M) \times (S + W)$$

In developing a formula for measuring and comparing national power, it is clear that calculations based solely on population and territory would be misleading unless adjusted to show particular economic strengths developed by the people in managing the resources of the land. In other words, the formula $P_p = C$ is too crude a measure; the equation is more useful—although still incomplete—if it reads $P_p = C + E$. What the people of a country have actually accomplished, or could presumably accomplish in short order, with their material and spiritual wealth, is a critical factor in their own and others' perceptions of their power. Economic strength is the basis on which a nation satisfies the needs of its people for goods and services, and also on which it is able to build its organized military capabilities, to manufacture arms, to supply manpower, and to provide the logistic and technical support needed by modern armies, navies, and air forces. Through investment and trade, nations help to enrich one another, and standards of living depend not only on the efficiency of national economic activity but also on access to resources and markets through international commerce. The next task in our assessment of world power is therefore to look at countries from the economic viewpoint. While here as elsewhere we are dealing with macrometrics designed to support general conclusions, some greater precision in quantification is possible.

The task of measurement is not easy, however, because economic strength is a multidimensional concept with many different insights into different aspects of those economic facts of life which contribute to a broad perception of overall performance. Current economic output and wealth, which are functions of both resources and the form and effectiveness of economic organization, are all-important at moments of imminent conflict or threat, because they represent an immediate ability to respond. Over a long period of time, economic potential, which is partly a function of reserve capabilities, is especially critical for maintaining a high level of economic activity, as well as for supporting military strength during a long confrontation or conflict. The economic potential for military effort in war or short-of-war conflicts is also affected by the ease and efficiency with which resources and available capacity can be reallocated to different needs, such as the production of more submarines or intercontinental missiles in place of a greater variety of passenger automobiles.

Another qualification concerning perceptions of current economic capacity is that it may depend, often precariously, on a nation's trade relations with the rest of the world, which supplies it with either raw materials or markets for goods produced. So long as the nation-state is the primary actor, nations that are more self-sufficient than others—especially in terms of essential goods such as raw materials for industry and foodstuffs—are probably perceived, rightly or wrongly, to be more powerful than others with the same level of current economic capacity.

In advanced industrial societies in peacetime, however, this self-sufficiency is more a liability, a sacrifice of economic benefits, than an asset. In times when international trade flows safely, nations that control a large share of the world's trade and investment not only improve the standard of living of their own people but also are able to exercise substantial power over other nations that want goods or capital. While the self-sufficiency of the domestic economy in critical categories is an asset, so is the leverage that foreign trade and investment can give.

Finally, what may be important economically for one country may not be so for another. Production of cement in the poorest nations is a measure of industrial strength, but, for the developed countries, the production of other more technologically complex goods is much more advantageous. Thus the use of quantitative measures of economic capability must be tempered by an understanding of countries at various stages of economic development. In this study, indicators have been selected to reflect a broad and balanced range of factors but also to stress the capability of one nation to exert an influence on other nations in short-of-war conflicts or confrontations.

Measurement of Economic Capability: GNP

The most comprehensive way of calculating the extent of a country's mobilized economic strength is to assess the total value of economic goods and services produced and marketed annually, that is, the gross national product (GNP). If qualified with appropriate caveats about other aspects of a nation's economic structure, particularly its natural resources, its technological skills, and its international trade, comparisons among nations based on GNP are extremely revealing. Furthermore, GNP is a standard of concrete measurement made familiar to decision makers and much of the public in open societies through repeated worldwide use by the information media.

The GNP is not just a gauge of material availabilities because volume and growth of the GNP include services affecting the quality of life and point to a nation's organizational and technological abilities, its brainpower directed at economic development. The initial economic analysis in this chapter is based on estimated GNP data for the calendar year 1978. In terms of power perception, the use of recent, reliably researched, estimated data is preferable to either finalized, accurate, but out-of-date or "soft," projected data for the current year. The decision makers in national government necessarily use estimated and preliminary data in much the same way and are seldom more up-to-date on firm quantitative ground than readers of this book when broad strategic plans are being evolved.

The GNP will vary over time with business conditions; the ratio between the GNPs of several countries experiencing a similar prosperity or recession will remain unchanged from year to year except in the decimals that are deceptive of reliability under any circumstances. On the whole, GNP ratios fluctuate little over periods of a few years and sometimes not even in the long-term. There are, however, exceptions either in real life or in its statistical reflection. Lebanon's GNP was actually cut in half in 1975-1976; it bounced back by an estimated 40 percent in 1977 and is currently again in difficulty. Such disturbances are serious for the people affected, but the GNPs of Lebanon or Ethiopia or Kampuchea do not much affect the global relationship considered in this book. The combined GNPs of the OPEC (Organization of Petroleum Exporting Countries) community did in reality increase two and one-half fold between 1973 and 1974 as a result of rising oil prices. This represented a highly unusual transfer of purchasing power from oil importers to oil suppliers. Examples of long-term changes are the "economic miracle" of Japan on the positive side and Great Britain's *mal anglais* on the negative side. If in a particular year the United States should be in a recession while the USSR enjoys a bountiful harvest, the Soviet-U.S. GNP ratio will rise; the following year it may dip again.

What quickly emerges from an examination of these data is that most of the world's activity resulting in measurable economic goods and services takes place in a relatively small number of countries. Among these, the United States is altogether in a class by itself. The 1978 GNP of the United States went over the two trillion rate, that is, $2,000 billion, an all-time high for any nation. If you compare this rate with 1975 figures, it is clear it represents more inflation than real economic growth. The 1979 statistics suggest a GNP of about $2.3 trillion, an amount that includes a high rate of inflation.

Nonetheless the United States alone produced and disposed of a little more than one-fourth of the world product in 1978. The nine nations with the largest GNPs account for nearly three-fourths of the world's economic output. It is noteworthy that all but the USSR and the PRC are close allies of the United States. The top forty-seven nations ranked according to critical mass of population and territory in Table 3 account for well over 90 percent of the economic goods and services produced in the entire world.

Variations in economic strength as measured by GNP are sometimes more apparent than real, since they may be purely statistical. The dollar currently is undervalued in relation to several Western currencies and to the Japanese yen. This fact increases the GNP ratio for, say, West Germany or Switzerland and Japan vis-à-vis the United States at present official exchange rates. This kind of shift in comparative standing does not affect the real economic strength of these countries, though it does alter the prestige of their currencies (a matter not to be overlooked). For example, it appears that in 1979, partly due to this dollar conversion factor, Japan will be the second largest economy in the world, going over the one trillion level—just a little higher than the USSR. The GNPs of less-developed countries are always understated for complicated reasons involving the difficulty of indexing price comparisons over space and time. The best solution, given the present state of the art, is probably the application of purchasing power equivalents; the GNPs of the Warsaw Pact nations are actually based on purchasing power equivalents. There is no good statistical base for calculating the GNP of the PRC, but the flood of admissions of shortcomings from Peking in the past year has led me to adopt the Central Intelligence Agency's (CIA) estimate for 1977 as close to the real GNP for 1978. The economic strength of the less-developed countries is actually somewhat greater than the GNP, converted at official rates of exchange, indicates. Even when this factor is taken into account, the weight of less-developed countries in the world economy is small, much smaller probably than the political and strategic weight conventionally attributed to them.

There is a common tendency to perceive economic power, at least partially, as a function of the rate of development – a tendency that may become radically altered by resource dependencies. The ranking system employed for GNP is straightforward; it assigns a score or weight of one hundred for the highest ranking country, the United States, and proportionately lesser scores to nations with smaller GNPs. This preliminary ranking will be adjusted and refined after we examine additional economic details specific to each country. By including all nations with a 1978 GNP of U.S. $10 billion or more, we create a list of fifty-six nations in Table 5, including most, although not all, of the countries ranking high in critical mass.

Special Economic Strengths and Weaknesses

As an aggregate measure, GNP necessarily conceals many special features in an economy. Some of these strengths and weaknesses have a substantial impact on the perceived image of national power in international relations.

For this reason, I have selected five broad factors to modify or adjust the GNP-based rankings. They are energy, critical minerals, industrial strength, food production, and foreign trade. Because perceived power is a relative concept by which nations compare themselves, or are compared, to other nations, these special characteristics are for the most part measured relative to an international standard of economic performance.

Each country is assigned an additional value for each of these supplemental measures of economic strength, with a possible additional total of 100 weight units, or 20 for each special economic strength. These values may be viewed as bonus economic weights above and beyond GNP. In a few cases of otherwise economically powerful nations, specific weaknesses are so apparent that a negative value must be taken into account – by subtracting units of power weights from the overall economic total.

Table 5. Gross National Product, 1978[7]
(in billions of U.S. dollars)

The 56 Leading Countries	GNP	Perceived Power Weights*
1. United States	2,025.0	100
2. USSR	973.1	49
3. Japan	695.1	34
4. Germany (FRG)	490.9	24
5. France	393.6	19
6. China (PRC)	375.0	18
7. United Kingdom	249.7	12
8. Italy	202.0	10
9. Canada	189.6	9
10. Brazil	130.6	6
11. India	120.5	6
12. Spain	110.8	5
13. Poland	108.3	5
14. Australia	95.3	5
15. Netherlands	89.3	4
16. Iran	87.6	4
17. Germany (GDR)	81.0	4
18. Saudi Arabia	71.2	4
19. Czechoslovakia	70.7	3
20. Sweden	69.8	3
21. Belgium–Luxembourg	68.6	3
22. Mexico	68.0	3
23. Rumania	67.4	3
24. Switzerland	55.3	3
25. Yugoslavia	49.4	2
26. Argentina	42.9	2
27. Austria	42.1	2
28. Turkey	42.0	2
29. Indonesia	41.9	2
30. Denmark	40.6	2
31. South Africa	39.1	2
32. Korea, South	39.0	2
33. Nigeria	38.5	2
34. Norway	32.2	2
35. Hungary	32.1	2
36. Venezuela	28.0	1
37. Finland	27.6	1
38. Bulgaria	24.8	1
39. Greece	24.2	1
40. China/Taiwan	24.1	1
41. Iraq	22.9	1
42. Algeria	22.2	1
43. Thailand	21.9	1
44. Kuwait	17.9	1
45. Pakistan	17.9	1

Table 5. (Cont.)

The 56 Leading Countries	GNP	Perceived Power Weights*
46. Philippines	17.8	1
47. Portugal	17.0	1
48. Colombia	16.2	1
49. Libya	16.1	1
50. Egypt	16.0	1
51. Israel	16.0	1
52. New Zealand	15.4	1
53. Chile	14.8	1
54. Peru	14.2	1
55. Bangladesh	11.6	1
56. Malaysia	10.4	1
Total	7,725.2	

*The United States, with a GNP of $2,025.0 billion, is allocated a maximum power weight of 100. All other nations are rated proportionately.

Energy

Clearly, energy is one of the most vital components of economic power, particularly in highly industrialized countries, and in those nonindustrial nations that control energy resources. Current energy consumption is, of course, closely correlated with the level of GNP, and to some extent has already been measured. But one special aspect of energy can easily and profoundly affect both present and potential economic and military power; it is energy adequacy or—in the negative case—dependency.

As the 1973-1974 oil embargo demonstrated, the need to rely on foreign suppliers of energy may seriously constrain economic activity in times of shortages. Countries that must import large quantities of energy have a more precarious economic base than ones that rely primarily on domestic sources. Conversely, countries producing a surplus of energy, which they export, have under such conditions leverage over some other nations. This fact the oil-producing cartel has ably exploited. Table 6 for petroleum assigns

Table 6. Petroleum, 1978[8]

Country	Production	Estimated Supply (in millions of barrels per day)			Estimated Capacity (in millions of barrels)		
		Exports Available*	Imports Required	Perceived Power Weights	Reserves**	Bonus	Total Perceived Power Weights†
1. Saudi Arabia	8.1§	8.1	—	8	166,000	2	10
2. Iran	3.0††	3.0	—	3	59,000	2	5
3. USSR	11.4	3.0	—	3	50,000	2	5
4. Kuwait	1.9	1.9	—	2	66,000	2	4
5. Iraq	2.5	2.5	—	2	32,000	1	3
6. Venezuela	2.2	2.2	—	2	18,000	1	3
7. Libya	2.0	2.0	—	2	24,000	1	3
8. Nigeria	1.9	1.9	—	2	18,000	1	3
9. United Arab Emirates	1.8	1.8	—	2	32,000	1	3
10. Indonesia	1.6	1.6	—	1	10,000	1	2
11. Algeria	1.1	1.1	—	1	6,000	0	1
12. Mexico	1.3	0.3	—	0	16,000	1	1
13. China (PRC)	2.0	0.2	—	0	20,000	1	1

Table 6. (Cont.)

| Country | Estimated Supply (in millions of barrels per day) | | | | Estimated Capacity (in millions of barrels) | | |
	Production	Exports Available*	Imports Required	Perceived Power Weights	Reserves**	Bonus Power Weights	Total Perceived Power Weights†
14. Canada	1.6	—	.50	0	6,000	0	0
15. United Kingdom	1.1	—	.80	-1	16,000	1	0
16. Italy	.28	—	1.72	-2	y	0	-2
17. Germany (FRG)	1.0	—	1.9	-2	y	0	-2
18. France	.21	—	2.19	-2	y	0	-2
19. Japan	.10	—	5.30	-5	y	0	-5
20. United States	10.3	—	9.44	-9	29,000	1	-8

y = negligible

§As an accommodation to the United States, Saudi production was raised in 1979 to 9.5 million barrels per day, but it is not clear how long this rate will be maintained.

*In many of the oil-producing states domestic consumption is negligible and virtually total production is available for export.

**Reserves are estimated *proved* oil reserves as of January 1979, and are subject to fairly rapid change.

†Total perceived power weights are allocated on a proportional basis with a maximum value of 10 points, 8 for production and 2 (bonus) for proved reserves.

††Estimated production as a result of curtailments due to Khomeini revolution. Production in 1978, prior to the revolution, was at the rate of 5.2 million barrels per day.

Source: Petroleum production and export figures primarily from National Foreign Assessment Center. *The World Oil Market in the Years Ahead.* August, 1979.

power points to reflect in a general way the volume of current national production, exports available, or imports required, on a net basis. Among the four primary energy sources—oil, coal, natural gas, and nuclear power—maximum weights are set at 10, 2, 4, and 4 respectively. Bonus points are added for proven petroleum reserves where appropriate. The predominant position of oil in these calculations is due not only to its status as the most important source of world energy consumption, but also to the fact that it is by far the main fuel commodity moving in world trade. It is, as well, an indispensable requirement for modern military forces.

Oil has been highly publicized as a crucial natural resource since the 1973 embargo, and it impinges very directly on the consumer at the gasoline pump as well as on the industrial producer. Having a sufficient supply of oil is one of the most difficult problems for the United States, economically and strategically. Although the United States is one of the world's largest producers of oil, it is alone among major producers in also requiring massive imports to meet its economic needs. The USSR may reach the stage of requiring imports in a few years, and this makes the inexpensively produced oil of the Arabian peninsula and Persian Gulf strategically a valuable prize for the next decade before alternative fuels can possibly be developed sufficiently to meet world demand.

This information on the sufficiency of energy in major countries, based on oil production, consumption, and export/import data, must be corrected by some allowance for supplies of the other fossil fuels, coal and natural gas. These have been much less exported and hence less noted as sources of energy. Yet they are still widely used and essential in most modern economies, probably increasingly so as oil supplies become less adequate to meet demand. Nuclear power capacity must also be taken into account.

Tables 7 and 8 list the major coal and natural gas producers, and the countries principally involved in the international trade of those commodities.

There is one more element in energy production looming large in the future and even larger in the public perception of its importance, and that is nuclear energy. Here the picture is straightforward. The industry is in its infancy. The United States is far in the lead, although environmental and safety considerations are for the time being slowing down plans for future growth. At present, nuclear energy accounts for something on the order of 1 to 2 percent of international energy production. There are over 200 nuclear power reac-

Table 7. Coal, 1978[9]
(in millions of tons)

Country	Production	Exports	Imports	Perceived Power Weights*
1. Poland	234.0	37.0	—	2
2. United States	619.0	34.2	—	2
3. USSR	612.0	17.2	—	1
4. South Africa	91.0	15.4	—	1
5. Australia	91.0	12.5	—	1
6. Germany (FRG)	126.0	12.4	—	1
7. China (PRC)**	600.0	2.0	—	0
8. India	106.0	y	—	0
9. United Kingdom	122.0	—	0.1	0
10. Denmark	y	—	4.2	0
11. Netherlands	y	—	4.5	0
12. Spain	16.0	—	5.0	0
13. Bulgaria	y	—	6.2	0
14. Germany (GDR)	y	—	6.5	0
15. Belgium–Luxembourg	7.0	—	6.9	0
16. Italy	y	—	13.0	−1
17. France	22.0	—	22.9	−1
18. Japan	19.0	—	52.2	−4

y = negligible

*A maximum of 2 power weights is assigned to the largest coal exporters, and other nations are ranked according to the amount of coal exports or import requirements. While availability of coal as an alternate form of energy for domestic consumption is an important indicator of general economic strength and is counted as such in the GNP calculations, in the international context, exports and imports are visible signs of extra resources of energy dependency.

**Includes some lignite.

tors now operating worldwide, with about as many more under construction or planned.

Cost factors and construction delays due to environmental concerns in some nations, especially the United States, have kept the world nuclear energy component a minor factor. The dynamics of the situation and the sheer fascination of the public with nuclear energy, however, suggest that some economic points must be added to a calculation of economic strength in the energy field to account for technological progress in constructing nuclear reactors. Perceived power weights calculated in Table 9 are in proportion to radiated megawattage, allowing the United States a maximum of 4.

Table 8. Natural Gas, 1977[10]
(in billions of cubic feet)

Country	Marketed Production*	Exports	Imports	Perceived Power Weights**
1. Netherlands	3,422	1,995	—	4
2. Canada	3,161	998	—	2
3. USSR	12,219	467	—	1
4. Iran	748	327	—	1
5. Japan	98	—	382	-1
6. Belgium–Luxembourg	1	—	422	-1
7. Italy	485	—	584	-1
8. France	272	—	503	-1
9. United States	20,025	—	955	-2
10. Germany (FRG)	638	—	941	-2

*Marketed production includes all gas collected and used as a fuel or as a chemical industry raw material as well as that used for gas lift in fields, including gas used in oil fields and/or gas fields as a fuel by producers. It does not include gas vented, flared, reinjected for repressurizing or for storage and used to drive gas turbines without being burned.

**Natural gas is an energy commodity of growing importance in international trade. A maximum of 4 power weights is assigned to the leading exporter and other nations are ranked according to the amount of gas exports or import requirements. Brunei, a British protectorate, marketed 314 billion cubic feet of natural gas in 1977 and exported 289 billion cubic feet; although it is therefore a major exporter, it is not an independent nation and is excluded from the table, where it would have been ranked fifth.

From all of these data it was possible to construct Table 10 giving the total points for general perceived power weights in the energy field. Petroleum availability is the prime consideration, but dependency is modified in some cases by possession of coal, natural gas, and nuclear reactors.

Table 9. Nuclear Power, 1978[11]

Country	Operating Reactors*	Effective Radiated Megawattage	Perceived Power Weights**
1. United States	69	49,914	4
2. Japan	18	12,200	2
3. USSR	22	8,475	2
4. United Kingdom	33	8,470	2
5. Germany (FRG)	12	7,335	2
6. Canada	9	4,736	2
7. France	14	4,498	2
8. Sweden	7	3,700	1
9. Belgium-Luxembourg	3	1,650	1
10. Germany (GDR)	3	1,390	1
11. Italy	4	1,387	1
12. Spain	4	1,073	1
13. Switzerland	3	1,020	1
14. Bulgaria	2	880	1
15. China/Taiwan	1	604	1
16. India	3	602	1
17. Korea, South	1	564	1
18. Netherlands	2	493	1
19. Finland	1	420	1
20. Argentina	1	320	1
21. Pakistan	1	125	1
22. Czechoslovakia	1	110	1

*The type of fuel used, enrichment facilities available, and the reactors under construction also influence perceived power with regard to nuclear energy, but an adequate examination of such additional factors are beyond the general assessment approach of this book.

**Power weights in this table are assigned in rough proportion to effective megawattage. While nuclear power plays an exceedingly small role in terms of overall world energy consumption, it nonetheless confers a special status reflected above by a maximum value of four power weights. The United States, clearly far superior in number of operating reactors and megawatts, is limited to an arbitrary maximum value of 4 since its energy requirements are sufficiently large to absorb the benefits of this lead and since U.S. policy on further development of nuclear energy for power is in a state of paralysis due to environmental concerns.

Table 10. Energy Assessment, 1978
(perceived power weights)

Country	Petroleum	Coal	Natural Gas	Nuclear	Total
1. Saudi Arabia	10	—	—	—	10
2. USSR	5	1	1	2	9
3. Iran	5	—	1	—	6
4. Netherlands	—	—	4	1	5
5. Kuwait	4	—	—	—	4
6. Canada	—	—	2	2	4
7. Venezuela	3	—	—	—	3
8. Iraq	3	—	—	—	3
9. Nigeria	3	—	—	—	3
10. Libya	3	—	—	—	3
11. United Arab Emirates	3	—	—	—	3
12. Poland	—	2	—	—	2
13. Indonesia	2	—	—	—	2
14. United Kingdom	—	—	—	2	2
15. Australia	—	1	—	—	1
16. Sweden	—	—	—	1	1
17. China (PRC)	1	—	—	—	1
18. India	—	—	—	1	1
19. Mexico	1	—	—	—	1
20. Algeria	1	—	—	—	1
21. Switzerland	—	—	—	1	1
22. China/Taiwan	—	—	—	1	1
23. Korea, South	—	—	—	1	1
24. Finland	—	—	—	1	1
25. Argentina	—	—	—	1	1
26. Pakistan	—	—	—	1	1
27. Czechoslovakia	—	—	—	1	1
28. Spain	—	—	—	1	1
29. Bulgaria	—	—	—	1	1
30. Germany (GDR)	—	—	—	1	1
31. South Africa	—	1	—	—	1
32. Belgium–Luxembourg	—	—	-1	1	0
33. Germany (FRG)	- 2	1	-2	2	- 1
34. France	- 2	-1	-1	2	- 2
35. Italy	- 2	-1	-1	1	- 3
36. United States	- 8	2	-2	4	- 4
37. Japan	- 5	-4	-1	2	- 8

Critical Nonfuel Minerals

Some nonfuel minerals are in short supply to meet the needs of advanced industrial technology. Here the relevant measure is not total production so much as the adequacy of a nation's production for its domestic uses. The high consumption of these minerals is already in part measured by the level of GNP and the degree of industrial capacity. Heavy reliance on foreign sources is commonly perceived as a disadvantage to a nation. On the other hand, if it possesses or has control over critical minerals that other nations need, then it will derive economic leverage from this situation.

Five nonfuel minerals are especially critical because of their widespread use in modern industry: iron ore, copper,

Table 11. Iron Ore, 1978[12]
(in millions of metric tons)

Country	Production	Exports	Imports	Perceived Power Weights*
1. Australia	90	79	—	8
2. Brazil	66	58	—	6
3. USSR	244	41	—	4
4. Canada	42	27	—	3
5. India	38	22	—	2
6. Sweden	21	19	—	2
7. Liberia	29	18	—	2
8. Venezuela	13	12	—	1
9. China (PRC)	70	y	—	0
10. France	33	—	3	0
11. United Kingdom	4	—	15	-1
12. Belgium-Luxembourg	1	—	24	-2
13. United States	82	—	30	-3
14. Germany (FRG)	2	—	42	-4
15. Japan	1	—	115	-11

y = negligible

*The leading nation in iron ore trade, in this case an importer (Japan), is allocated -11 points. Other nations are proportionately weighted, with the top exporter, Australia, receiving the maximum weight of 8.

bauxite, chromite, and uranium. We treat iron ore as a special case with extra weight because its use is basic and widespread, particularly in heavy industry and military weapons manufacture. As with energy, exports of minerals from a country are treated as positive strength factors, and substantial imports are treated as negative values because of the dependency they reflect. Accordingly, in Table 11 countries are assigned economic points, plus or minus, in proportion to their surplus production or import requirement. With respect to iron ore, the maximum perceived power weight is set at 8, and weights are allocated in proportion down to the largest importer, in this case Japan, which receives a negative weight of 11.

Table 12. Copper, 1978[13]
(in thousands of metric tons)

Country	Production	Exports*	Imports*	Perceived Power Weights**
1. Chile	1,036	977.8	—	3
2. Zambia	643	575.5	—	2
3. Canada	658	462.5	—	2
4. Zaire	423	413.0	—	2
5. Peru	366	320.0	—	1
6. Philippines	239	239.0	—	1
7. USSR	865	140.0	—	1
8. Poland	290	165.0	—	1
9. Brazil	1,352	—	155.9	−1
10. Belgium–Luxembourg	y	—	252.2	−1
11. United States	y	—	272.4	−1
12. France	y	—	272.7	−1
13. Italy	y	—	353.9	−1
14. United Kingdom	y	—	394.4	−1
15. Germany (FRG)	y	—	536.9	−2
16. Japan	y	—	1,125.4	−3

y = negligible

*Estimates of exports and imports include ores and concentrates, blister, and refined copper, all in terms of copper content.

**The leading nation in copper trade, Chile, is allocated the maximum weight of 3 points; other nations are proportionately weighted.

The other four minerals—although less important than iron ore—are essential for some specialized types of manufacturing. They are scattered among different regions, and, in most cases, given time, could in emergencies be recycled or replaced with substitutes. Copper conductors, aluminum, and chrome alloys are integral to many light and heavy industries; uranium is increasingly prized as the world thinks of turning to nuclear reactors for its energy. Net exports are

Table 13. Bauxite, 1978[14]
(in thousands of metric tons)

Country	Production	Exports*	Imports*	Perceived Power Weights**
1. Australia	24,300	22,400	—	3
2. Guinea	12,064	12,064	—	1
3. Jamaica	11,736	10,756	—	1
4. Surinam	4,920	4,700	—	1
5. Guyana	3,450	3,450	—	0
6. Hungary	2,904	2,600	—	0
7. Greece	2,384	1,800	—	0
8. Yugoslavia	2,566	1,575	—	0
9. France	1,989	—	1,484	0
10. United Kingdom	y	—	1,713	0
11. Norway	y	—	2,600	0
12. Germany (FRG)	y	—	3,900	-1
13. Canada	y	—	4,479	-1
14. USSR	6,180	—	5,800	-1
15. Japan	y	—	6,211	-1
16. United States	1,669	—	20,858	-3

y = negligible

*Exports and imports include bauxite equivalent of alumina.

**The leading nation in bauxite trade, Australia, is allocated the maximum weight of 3 points; other nations are proportionately weighted.

calculated as positive factors and imports are treated as negative factors, assigning weights based on the primacy of iron ore with the other four minerals individually weighted. The maximum values are set at 8, 3, 3, 3, and 3 for iron ore, copper, bauxite, chromite, and uranium respectively. Tables 12, 13, 14, and 15 cover copper, bauxite, chromite, and uranium.

The total values for perceived power weights of nations with respect to the five critical nonfuel minerals appear in Table 16.

Table 14. Chromite,* 1978[15]
(in thousands of metric tons)

Country	Production	Exports	Imports	Perceived Power Weights**
1. South Africa	3,455	3,300	—	3
2. Albania	900	890	—	1
3. USSR	2,300	800	—	1
4. Turkey	700	690	—	1
5. Zimbabwe–Rhodesia	600	600	—	1
6. Philippines	533	533	—	1
7. India	257	237	—	0
8. Italy	y	—	246	0
9. France	y	—	401	0
10. Sweden	y	—	469	−1
11. Germany (FRG)	y	—	615	−1
12. Japan	y	—	882	−1
13. United States	y	—	1,560	−2

y = negligible

*Includes chromite equivalent of ferro-chromite traded.

**The leading nation in chromite trade, South Africa, is allocated the maximum weight of 3 points; other nations are proportionately weighted.

Table 15. Uranium, 1978[16]
(in metric tons U_3O_8)

Country	Production*	Perceived Power Weights
1. United States	15,013	3
2. USSR	**	2
3. Canada	9,440	2
4. South Africa (including Namibia)	8,130	1
5. France	2,400	1
6. Niger	1,830	0
7. Gabon	726	0
8. Australia	609	0

*Owing to the sensitive uses for uranium in weapons and energy production, and due to the individual complexities of uranium trade, reliable export/import data are not readily available and are not produced here. Power weights are based on production data alone which, in the specific case of uranium, may well be a better indicator of perceived power.

**Soviet uranium production, which probably includes the production of several East European Communist states, is not reported outside the USSR but is estimated to be perhaps one-half to two-thirds of U.S. production. Because of this uncertainty, no production figure is listed but an appropriate power weight is assessed.

Table 16. Critical Nonfuel Minerals Assessment, 1978 (perceived power weights)

Country	Iron Ore	Copper	Bauxite	Chromite	Uranium	Total
1. Australia	8	—	3	—	—	11
2. USSR	4	1	-1	1	2	7
3. Canada	3	2	-1	—	2	6
4. Brazil	6	-1	—	—	—	5
5. South Africa	—	—	—	3	1	4
6. Chile	—	3	—	—	—	3
7. Philippines	—	1	—	1	—	2
8. Zaire	—	2	—	—	—	2
9. Zambia	—	2	—	—	—	2
10. India	2	—	—	—	—	2
11. Liberia	2	—	—	—	—	2
12. Guinea	—	—	1	—	—	1
13. Jamaica	—	—	1	—	—	1
14. Peru	—	1	—	—	—	1
15. Poland	—	1	—	—	—	1
16. Surinam	—	—	1	—	—	1
17. Albania	—	—	—	1	—	1
18. Turkey	—	—	—	1	—	1
19. Zimbabwe–Rhodesia	—	—	—	1	—	1
20. Venezuela	1	—	—	—	—	1
21. Sweden	2	—	—	-1	—	1
22. France	—	-1	—	—	1	0
23. Italy	—	-1	—	—	—	- 1
24. United Kingdom	- 1	-1	—	—	—	- 2
25. Belgium-Luxembourg	- 2	-1	—	—	—	- 3
26. United States	- 3	-1	-3	-2	3	- 6
27. Germany (FRG)	- 4	-2	-1	-1	—	- 8
28. Japan	-11	-3	-1	-1	—	-16

Industry

Industrial strength is closely associated with a nation's economic capability, since it represents that nation's ability to fabricate the basic materials of heavy manufacturing, machine tools, many consumer goods, and, of course, military hardware. For the past century the predominant place in industry has been held by steel. It goes into almost everything that builds manufacturing capability, and steel plants always have a high priority in developing nations. The gross magnitude of national steel production is one of the most appropriate measurements of the power of an industrial nation.[17] Only a postindustrial society like the United States can turn to services and quality-of-life production as more expensive elements of its economy.

The United States has installed plant capacity in the steel industry so large that it can satisfy manufacturing needs easily. Self-sufficiency in steel was in a sense assessed earlier by the variable dealing with a nation's dependency on importing iron ore for its supply of this critical mineral. In any case, it is the level of steel production that other nations consider in assessing the industrial might of adversaries or allies, particularly because of its importance in manufacturing heavy military weapons and equipment.

Production of aluminum, an additional metal industry, can be used as an economic indicator of light industry and consumers' equipment manufacturing capabilities. Here, too, the gross magnitude of national production is a good index of performance, and self-sufficiency has already in a sense been assessed by looking at the relatively few nations producing bauxite on a large scale.

A third indicator of industrial capability, especially initial industrial capability, is in the manufacture of building materials, the most important of which is cement. Treating steel as central, additional points are assigned on a basis that sets 10 as a maximum allowance for steel production and 5 each as a maximum allowance for aluminum and cement production. On this basis Tables 17, 18, and 19 rank nations in their production of steel, aluminum, and cement. Table 20 represents a composite for 1978 industrial strength.

Table 17. Crude Steel Production, 1978[18]
(in millions of metric tons)

Country	Production	Perceived Power Weights*
1. USSR	125.8	10
2. United States	103.2	8
3. Japan	85.0	7
4. Germany (FRG)	34.3	3
5. China (PRC)	26.0	2
6. Italy	20.2	2
7. France	19.0	2
8. United Kingdom	16.9	1
9. Poland	16.0	1
10. Czechoslovakia	12.7	1
11. Canada	12.4	1
12. Belgium–Luxembourg	10.5	1
13. Brazil	10.2	1
14. Spain**	9.3	1
15. India	8.0	1

*The leading producer, the USSR, is allocated a maximum of 10 points with other producers proportionately weighted.

**The figure for Spain is extrapolated.

Table 18. Aluminum Production, 1978[19]
(in millions of metric tons)

Country	Production*	Perceived Power Weights**
1. United States	430.0	5
2. Japan	112.0	1
3. USSR	102.0	1
4. Germany (FRG)	96.0	1
5. Norway	53.3	1
6. United Kingdom	44.9	1
7. France	44.5	1

*Production figures include primary and secondary aluminum production. The USSR estimate does not include secondary production. While this would increase production somewhat, it should not be sufficient to change the USSR power weight. Canadian production figures are not available since June 1976 and are therefore not included in this list.

**The leading producer, the United States, is allocated a maximum of 5 points. Other producers are proportionately weighted, although the last three major producers are given a whole unit of 1 weight rather than the fraction that would be truly in proportion.

Table 19. Cement Production, 1978[20]
(in millions of metric tons)

Country	Production	Perceived Power Weights*
1. USSR	107.7	5
2. Japan	70.7	4
3. United States	59.8	3
4. China (PRC)	40.0	2
5. Italy	32.0	1
6. Germany (FRG)	27.9	1
7. Spain	24.4	1
8. France	23.4	1
9. Brazil	18.4	1
10. Poland	18.0	1
11. India	16.3	1
12. Korea, South	14.1	1
13. United Kingdom	13.3	1
14. Mexico	11.9	1

*The leading producer, the USSR, is allocated a maximum of 5 points. Other producers are proportionately weighted.

Table 20. Industrial Production Assessment, 1978
(perceived power weights)

Country	Steel	Aluminum	Cement	Total
1. USSR	10	1	5	16
2. United States	8	5	3	16
3. Japan	7	1	4	12
4. Germany (FRG)	3	1	1	5
5. China (PRC)	2	—	2	4
6. France	2	1	1	4
7. Italy	2	—	1	3
8. United Kingdom	1	1	1	3
9. Poland	1	—	1	2
10. Brazil	1	—	1	2
11. Spain	1	—	1	2
12. India	1	—	1	2
13. Canada	1	—	—	1
14. Norway	—	1	—	1
15. Korea, South	—	—	1	1
16. Mexico	—	—	1	1
17. Belgium–Luxembourg	1	—	—	1
18. Czechoslovakia	1	—	—	1

Foods

The 1970s have repeatedly demonstrated that agricultural capacity may in the future be one of the most critical components of economic power. Nations that must import food suffer from the uncertainty of sometimes dealing in tight international markets. They may have to endure domestic disruptions if food is inadequate, and in any case use valuable foreign reserves that could otherwise purchase minerals, machines, technology, or weapons. On the other hand, nations that produce a surplus of food commodities are insulated from the vagaries of the climate and the international market (though not from their own farm lobbies). They also possess potential bargaining power in international relations if they choose to use it.

Although the effects of a strong or weak agriculture may be quite marked, objective and concise measurement of agricultural potential and capacity is not easy. Consideration of resources alone, such as arable land, is inadequate because the productivity of land varies so widely. For example, rice yields in Asia may be several times the yields in Africa. Land may be the fundamental factor of agricultural production, but its usefulness depends heavily on the corresponding climate, the amount of labor and machinery available to till it, and the level of chemical and biological technology applied to agricultural crops rather than to food production.

Consideration of output alone is also inadequate. For example, not all cereals are produced for human consumption. In the United States, over 50 percent of the total cereal growth is for animals; most of the animals, in turn, are raised for food. This agriculture-food pattern is inherently a less efficient producer of calories than a more primitive economic system in which cereal plants are consumed directly. To complicate matters, some countries, such as Argentina and Australia, have a relatively low cereal production, mostly for human consumption. Farmers in these countries add substantially to agricultural capacity by grazing large herds of cattle on natural grasslands that otherwise would be unproductive. A measurement based on cereals alone might understate the agricultural strength of these countries.

Furthermore, governments are usually heavily involved in the agricultural sector in most countries. Their intervention may cause distortions such as suppressing possible agricultural production, as was done in the United States for many years in order to maintain higher prices for the benefit of farmers. A measure based solely on current output would in this case understate real U.S. capacity.

Finally, any measures of agricultural production must be considered relative to a country's population. More heavily populated countries require more agricultural production; and greater density usually means there is more manpower for agriculture, which normally raises yields. The case of the People's Republic of China is relevant. The GNP of mainland China is based primarily on agriculture, and about 80 percent of the vast Chinese population lives in rural areas and subsists mainly by agricultural labor. The magnitude of this effort, nevertheless, produces no food surplus and the country, despite its size, is in no sense economically strong because of the necessity to employ the major part of its labor force in feeding the population at a mere subsistence level.

Table 21 lists the main agricultural trading nations, and examines exports and imports of the three major commodities – wheat, coarse grains, and rice – in metric tons. Small grains or root crops, such as potatoes, are not included and the fact that some grains are traded in the form of meat is not noted. These refinements are too complex for our broad purposes.

The benefit of this approach is its clear focus on the essential element of national power in the international environment. Countries that export foods possess economic advantages stemming from a high level of agricultural output, while countries that import foods are weak in comparison because they lack the leverage in international affairs that surplus foods provide in a frequently hungry world. The leading food-trading country, the United States, is assigned the maximum weight of 20 with other weights accorded proportionally. Only those states having a total net import/export

Table 21. Food, July 1976–June 1977[21]
(net exports [+]/imports [−]*, in millions of metric tons)

Country	Wheat	Coarse Grains	Rice	Total	Perceived Power Weights**
1. United States	+ 25.4	+ 51.5	+ 2.3	+ 79.2	20
2. Canada	+ 12.0	+ 3.9	− 0.1	+ 15.8	4
3. Argentina	+ 5.6	+ 8.8	+ 0.2	+ 14.6	4
4. Australia	+ 8.0	+ 3.5	+ 0.3	+ 11.8	3
5. France	+ 6.0	+ 0.4	− 0.2	+ 6.2	2
6. Thailand	− 0.1	+ 2.2	+ 2.9	+ 5.0	1
7. Netherlands	+ 0.2	+ 3.4	− 0.1	+ 3.5	1
8. South Africa	+ 0.3	+ 1.5	− 0.1	+ 1.7	0
9. Sweden	+ 0.9	+ 0.2	y	+ 1.1	0
10. Morocco	− 1.0	y	y	− 1.0	0
11. Bangladesh	− 0.5	y	− 0.5	− 1.0	0
12. Sri Lanka	− 0.5	y	− 0.5	− 1.0	0
13. Switzerland	− 0.3	− 0.9	y	− 1.2	0
14. Nigeria	− 0.7	y	− 0.5	− 1.2	0
15. Malaysia	− 0.4	− 0.3	− 0.5	− 1.2	0
16. Peru	− 0.9	− 0.5	y	− 1.4	0
17. Cuba	− 0.8	− 0.4	− 0.2	− 1.4	0
18. Mexico	y	− 1.5	y	− 1.5	0
19. Israel	− 0.5	− 1.1	y	− 1.6	0
20. Venezuela	− 0.7	− 1.0	y	− 1.7	0
21. Brazil	− 3.3	+ 1.2	+ 0.3	− 1.8	0
22. Iran	− 1.0	− 0.7	− 0.5	− 2.2	− 1
23. China/Taiwan	− 0.6	− 1.8	+ 0.2	− 2.2	− 1
24. Portugal	− 0.4	− 2.1	− 0.1	− 2.6	− 1
25. Czechoslovakia	− 1.4	− 1.2	− 0.1	− 2.7	− 1
26. Indonesia	− 1.1	y	− 2.0	− 3.1	− 1
27. Korea, South	− 1.8	− 1.4	− 0.1	− 3.3	− 1
28. Belgium − Luxembourg	− 0.4	− 3.1	− 0.1	− 3.6	− 1
29. India	− 3.7	y	y	− 3.7	− 1
30. Spain	y	− 4.4	+ 0.1	− 4.3	− 1
31. Germany (GDR)	− 1.7	− 2.7	y	− 4.4	− 1
32. Egypt	− 4.1	− 0.7	+ 0.2	− 4.6	− 1
33. China (PRC)	− 4.0	− 0.1	− 0.7	− 4.8	− 1
34. Poland	− 2.0	− 4.0	− 0.1	− 6.1	− 2
35. Germany (FRG)	y	− 6.6	− 0.1	− 6.7	− 2
36. Italy	− 1.4	− 6.1	+ 0.3	− 7.2	− 2
37. USSR	− 3.5	− 3.5	− 0.3	− 7.3	− 2
38. United Kingdom	− 3.7	− 5.3	− 0.2	− 9.2	− 2
39. Japan	− 5.5	− 15.5	y	− 21.0	− 5

y = negligible

*Includes countries exporting or importing more than one million metric tons.

**The major food-trading nation, the United States, is allocated 20 points and other nations are proportionately weighted.

balance of one million metric tons or more are included. The power weights do not assess cases where a government does not import sufficient food to feed its population. In those cases the analysis would in some way underestimate true dependence.

It has been observed that Marx was a "city boy," overstressing industry. In any event, the USSR with its system of nearly incentiveless collective farms has been unsuccessful in insuring an adequate grain supply to feed the population and at the same time achieve the more costly system of animal husbandry that would permit the standard of Soviet living to rise to support a nation of meat-eaters, as the people want and the Soviet government repeatedly promises. The PRC and India, which together have approximately 40 percent of the world population, are able to feed themselves only when harvests are good. If recent trends continue, the United States may be the only major food exporter in the years ahead. It stands out far above the rest now.

Trade

Domestic economic power in our day is inextricably interwoven with international trade, and it must be so evaluated. To some extent we have already taken foreign economic relations into account in dealing with energy dependency, critical mineral resources, and agricultural production. But because of steadily growing interdependency among national economies, every nation must factor into its perception of its own comparative economic capability some index that reflects overall strengths stemming from national participation in the world economy.

Foreign trade is a good indicator of power or leverage exercised in international economic relations. Leverage derives from domination of world trade in certain regions or in certain commodities, mainly through exporting sought-after goods and services; in some cases an essential bulk importer gets some leverage over its trading partners by providing a fundamental market. For example, an active trading nation like Japan participates in a wide array of markets across the

Table 22. World Trade, 1978[22]
(in billions of U.S. dollars)

Country	Exports	Imports	Total Trade	Perceived Power Weights*
1. United States	143.7	183.1	326.8	20
2. Germany (FRG)	142.2	121.8	264.0	16
3. Japan	98.4	79.9	178.3	11
4. France	79.4	81.8	161.2	10
5. United Kingdom	71.7	78.6	150.3	8
6. Italy	56.1	56.5	112.6	7
7. Netherlands	50.3	54.1	104.4	7
8. USSR	52.2	50.5	102.7	6
9. Belgium–Luxembourg	45.0	48.5	93.5	6
10. Canada	47.9	44.8	92.7	6
11. Saudi Arabia	37.9	24.1	62.0	4
12. Switzerland	23.6	23.8	47.4	3
13. Sweden	21.8	20.6	42.4	3
14. Iran	22.4	18.7	41.1	3
15. Spain	13.1	18.7	31.8	2
16. Poland	13.4	15.1	28.5	2
17. Australia	14.4	14.0	28.4	2
18. Austria	12.2	16.0	28.2	2
19. Germany (GDR)	13.3	14.6	27.9	2
20. Korea, South	12.7	15.1	27.8	2
21. Brazil	12.7	15.0	27.7	2
22. Denmark	11.9	14.8	26.7	2
23. Czechoslovakia	12.3	12.6	24.9	2
24. China/Taiwan	12.7	11.1	23.8	2
25. Singapore	10.1	13.0	23.1	2
26. Norway	10.0	11.4	21.4	2
27. South Africa	12.8	7.2	20.0	2
28. Nigeria	10.4	9.5	19.9	1
29. Venezuela	9..1	8.7	17.8	1
30. Indonesia**	10.4	6.1	16.5	1
31. Finland	8.6	7.9	16.5	1
32. Rumania†	8.0	7.8	15.8	1
33. Yugoslavia	5.7	10.0	15.7	1
34. Libya	9.5	5.9	15.4	1
35. Kuwait	10.5	4.3	14.8	1
36. Hungary	6.4	7.9	14.3	1
37. Bulgaria†	7.2	7.0	14.2	1
38. Iraq**	11.0	3.1	14.1	1
39. China (PRC)	7.6	6.4	14.0	1
40. India	6.4	7.4	13.8	1

Table 22. (Cont.)

Country	Exports	Imports	Total Trade	Perceived Power Weights*
41. Algeria	5.9	7.9	13.8	1
42. United Arab Emirates**	9.0	4.6	13.6	1
43. Malaysia	7.4	5.9	13.3	1
TOTAL TRADE OF 43 NATIONS listed above				$2,363 billion
TOTAL WORLD TRADE				$2,377 billion

*The leading country, the United States, is allocated the maxiumum of 20 points with other nations proportionately weighted.

**Export and import figures for Indonesia are extrapolated from period of January–September; only import figures for the United Arab Emirates and Iraq are so extrapolated.

†Figures are extrapolated from annual figures for the years 1974–1977.

globe and benefits from a remarkably extensive penetration in the business activities of foreigners. Japan is also a crucial market for many products it imports from other nations. If any country is the major supplier of some vital commodity to another, the former has economic leverage over the latter; alternatively, if a country is the major purchaser of another's primary export, it, too, has a certain kind of leverage.

Perceptions of nations as major traders contribute to an image of power that connotes not only economic productivity but also the ability to maintain access to resources, marketplaces, and lanes of commerce around the globe. The trade variable thus crudely represents a nation's influence as a supplier or user of the world's valued goods and services. Nations with a larger share of world trade are accordingly commonly perceived to have greater power in the world economy. A weighted ranklist in Table 22 shows the total turnover (exports plus imports) for the forty-three countries that conducted more than U.S. $10 billion worth of trade during 1978. The level of $10 billion was used as a base level since it includes major trading nations and represents approximately 0.5 percent of total world trade.

To recapitulate, Table 23 is a consolidated ranklist weighted for GNP and for the five special economic factors examined in this chapter.

Table 23. Economic Capability Assessment, 1978
(perceived power weights)

Country	GNP (100)	Energy (20)	Critical Minerals (20)	Industrial Production (20)	Food (20)	World Trade (20)	Total (200)
1. United States	100	– 4	– 6	16	20	20	146
2. USSR	49	9	7	16	– 2	6	85
3. Germany (FRG)	24	– 1	– 8	5	– 2	16	34
4. France	19	– 2	—	4	2	10	33
5. Canada	9	4	6	1	4	6	30
6. Japan	34	– 8	–16	12	– 5	11	28
7. China (PRC)	18	1	—	4	– 1	1	23
8. Australia	5	1	11	—	3	2	22
9. United Kingdom	12	2	– 2	3	– 2	8	21
10. Saudi Arabia	4	10	—	—	—	4	18
11. Netherlands	4	5	—	—	1	7	17
12. Brazil	6	—	5	2	—	2	15
13. Italy	10	– 3	– 1	3	– 2	7	14
14. Iran	4	6	—	—	– 1	3	12
15. India	6	1	2	2	– 1	1	11
16. Poland	5	2	1	2	– 2	2	11
17. Spain	5	1	—	2	– 1	2	10
18. South Africa	2	1	4	—	—	2	9
19. Sweden	3	1	1	—	—	2	9
20. Switzerland	3	1	—	—	—	3	8
21. Belgium –Luxembourg	3	—	– 3	1	– 1	3	7
22. Argentina	2	1	—	—	4	6	6
23. Venezuela	1	3	1	—	—	1	6

Table 23. (Cont.)

Country	GNP (100)	Energy (20)	Critical Minerals (20)	Industrial Production (20)	Food (20)	World Trade (20)	Total (200)
24. Czechoslovakia	3	1	-	1	-1	2	6
25. Nigeria	2	3	-	-	-	1	6
26. Kuwait	1	4	-	-	-	1	6
27. Germany (GDR)	4	1	-	-	-1	2	6
28. Mexico	3	1	-	-1	-	-	5
29. Korea, South	2	1	-	-1	-1	2	5
30. Iraq	1	3	-	-	-	1	5
31. Libya	1	3	-	-1	-	-	5
32. Norway	2	-	-	-	-	2	5
33. Indonesia	2	2	-	-	-1	1	4
34. Rumania	3	-	-	-	-	1	4
35. Austria	2	-	-	-	-	2	4
36. United Arab Emirates	-	3	3	-	-	1	4
37. Chile	1	-	3	-	-	-	4
38. Denmark	2	-	-	-	-	2	4
39. Yugoslavia	2	-	-	-	-	1	3
40. Hungary	2	-	-	-	-	1	3
41. Turkey	2	-	1	-	-	-	3
42. Philippines	1	-	2	-	-	-	3
43. Algeria	1	1	-	-	-	1	3
44. Finland	1	1	-	-	-	1	3
45. Bulgaria	1	1	-	-	-	-	3
46. China/Taiwan	1	1	-	-	-1	2	3
47. Thailand	1	-	-	-	-1	-	2

#	Country							
48.	Peru	1	—	1	—	—	—	2
49.	Pakistan	1	1	—	—	—	—	2
50.	Malaysia	1	—	—	—	—	1	2
51.	Zaire	—	—	2	—	—	—	2
52.	Zambia	—	—	2	—	—	—	2
53.	Singapore	—	—	—	—	—	2	2
54.	Liberia	—	—	2	—	—	2	2
55.	Greece	1	—	—	—	—	—	1
56.	Guinea	—	—	1	—	—	—	1
57.	Jamaica	1	—	1	—	—	—	1
58.	Colombia	1	—	—	—	—	—	1
59.	New Zealand	1	—	—	—	—	—	1
60.	Israel	1	—	—	—	—	—	1
61.	Bangladesh	1	—	1	—	—	—	1
62.	Surinam	—	—	1	—	—	—	1
63.	Albania	—	—	1	—	—	—	1
64.	Zimbabwe-Rhodesia	1	—	—	—	—	—	1
65.	Egypt	1	—	—	—	1	—	0
66.	Portugal	—	—	—	—	1	—	0

Perceived Power for Critical Mass
plus Economic Capability

Table 24 registers countries on our macrometric scale of international perceptions of power as a result not only of their critical mass of population and territory but also their economic capability.

We now have a ranklist in which thirty-eight nations have combined perceived power weights of 15 or more. These nations clearly appear to be leading actors on the international scene. At this point an analysis of the world distribution of power suggests some broad observations:

1. The United States is stronger than the USSR and towers above all others.
2. North America is naturally a rich and powerful zone because it contains three large nations.
3. West Europe is an extremely valuable piece of real estate, mainly because of the industrial technology and skills of the several major countries there.
4. The USSR alone looms large in comparison with every other area except North America and West Europe.
5. The People's Republic of China, despite its vast population, is a secondary power on the order of magnitude of Brazil, Canada, and Japan rather than a true equal of the United States and the Soviet Union.

If perceptions of world power derived exclusively from population, territory, and economic capability, the distribution of lasting elements of power around the globe would be accurately reflected in Table 25. In fact, of course, military capability, strategic purpose, and political skill in mobilizing national will affect power perceptions substantially, as subsequent chapters will demonstrate.

Table 24. Consolidated Ranklist,
Critical Mass and Economic Capabilities, 1978
(perceived power weights)

Country	Critical Mass	Economic Capability	Total
1. United States	100	146	246
2. USSR	100	85	185
3. China (PRC)	75	23	98
4. Brazil	80	15	95
5. Canada	56	30	86
6. Japan	44	28	72
7. Australia	50	22	72
8. Germany (FRG)	30	34	64
9. India	52	11	63
10. France	28	33	61
11. Indonesia	56	4	60
12. United Kingdom	29	21	50
13. Italy	29	14	43
14. Argentina	31	7	38
15. Spain	25	9	34
16. Mexico	27	5	32
17. South Africa	23	9	32
18. Iran	18	12	30
19. Philippines	27	3	30
20. Saudi Arabia	12	18	30
21. Turkey	26	3	29
22. Nigeria	22	6	28
23. Vietnam	28	—	28
24. Bangladesh	27	1	28
25. Pakistan	25	2	27
26. Egypt	25	—	25
27. Korea, South	20	5	25
28. Poland	14	10	24
29. Zaire	19	2	21
30. Algeria	17	3	20
31. Norway	15*	5	20
32. Thailand	17	2	19
33. Chile	15*	4	19
34. Sudan	18	—	18
35. China/Taiwan	14	3	17
36. Netherlands	—	17	17
37. New Zealand	15*	1	16
38. Libya	10	5	15
39. Ethiopia	14	—	14

Table 24. (Cont.)

Country	Critical Mass	Economic Capability	Total
40. Rumania	10	4	14
41. Denmark	10*	4	14
42. Burma	13	—	13
43. Yugoslavia	10	3	13
44. Peru	11	2	13
45. Sweden	5*	8	13
46. Colombia	11	1	12
47. Venezuela	5*	6	11
48. Morocco	10	—	10
49. Iraq	5*	5	10
50. Czechoslovakia	4	6	10
51. Germany (GDR)	4	6	10
52. Kenya	9	—	9
53. Tanzania	9	—	9
54. Mongolia	8	—	8
55. Finland	5*	3	8
56. Zambia	5*	2	7
57. Malaysia	5*	2	7
58. Switzerland	—	7	7
59. Belgium–Luxembourg	—	6	6
60. Zimbabwe–Rhodesia	5*	1	6
61. Guinea	5*	1	6
62. Kuwait	—	6	6
63. Greece	5*	1	6
64. Surinam	5*	1	6
65. Korea, North	5	—	5
66. Austria	—	4	4
67. United Arab Emirates	—	4	4
68. Hungary	—	3	3
69. Bulgaria	—	3	3
70. Singapore	—	2	2
71. Liberia	—	2	2
72. Jamaica	—	1	1
73. Israel	—	1	1
74. Albania	—	1	1
		Total	2,091

*Of the twenty-seven new countries added to this consolidated ranklist because of economic strengths, fourteen were too small in population and territory to qualify for inclusion in Table 3 but were assigned small weights in Table 2. These weights are here included and added to the total value of consolidated perceived weights for both critical mass and economic capability as their total perceived weights.

Table 25. Distribution of Perceived Power by Politectonic Zones, 1978 (critical mass and economic capabilities)

Politectonic Zone	Country	Perceived Power Weights	Zonal Total
I	United States	246	
	Canada	86	365
	Mexico	32	
	Jamaica	1	
II	USSR	185	
	Poland	24	
	Rumania	14	
	Germany (GDR)	10	
	Czechoslovakia	10	258
	Mongolia	8	
	Hungary	3	
	Bulgaria	3	
	Albania*	1	
III	China (PRC)	98	
	Vietnam	28	131
	Korea, North	5	
IV	Germany (FRG)	64	
	France	61	
	United Kingdom	50	
	Italy	43	
	Spain	34	
	Norway	20	
	Netherlands	17	
	Denmark	14	360
	Yugoslavia*	13	
	Sweden**	13	
	Finland**	8	
	Switzerland**	7	
	Belgium–Luxembourg	6	
	Greece	6	
	Austria**	4	

Table 25. (Cont.)

Politectonic Zone	Country	Perceived Power Weights	Zonal Total
V	Saudi Arabia	30	
	Iran	30	
	Turkey	29	
	Egypt	25	
	Algeria	20	
	Sudan	18	198
	Libya	15	
	Morocco	10	
	Iraq	10	
	Kuwait	6	
	United Arab Emirates	4	
	Israel	1	
VI	India	63	
	Bangladesh	28	118
	Pakistan	27	
VII	Indonesia	60	
	Philippines	30	
	Thailand	19	131
	Burma	13	
	Malaysia	7	
	Singapore	2	
VIII	Japan	72	
	Korea, South	25	114
	China/Taiwan	17	
IX	Brazil	95	
	Argentina	38	
	Chile	19	
	Peru	13	194
	Colombia	12	
	Venezuela	11	
	Surinam	6	

Table 25. (Cont.)

Politectonic Zone	Country	Perceived Power Weights	Zonal Total
X	South Africa	32	134
	Nigeria	28	
	Zaire	21	
	Ethiopia	14	
	Kenya	9	
	Tanzania	9	
	Zambia	7	
	Zimbabwe–Rhodesia	6	
	Guinea	6	
	Liberia	2	
XI	Australia	72	88
	New Zealand	16	
	Total for all zones (74 nations)		2,091

*Communist but not aligned with either the USSR or PRC.

**Committed to neutrality. The total of perceived weights for the other countries of West Europe, all with close relations to the United States, is 326.

CHAPTER FIVE

Military Capability: The Strategic Force Balance
$P_p = (C + E + M) \times (S + W)$

The ultimate sanction in disputes between nations is the use of military force. As von Clausewitz said, "War is a mere continuation of policy by other means; . . . an act of violence intended to compel our opponent to fulfill our will" by "the utmost use of force."[23]

Conflicts among nations usually start with political arguments and diplomatic pressures and proceed through the offering or withholding of increasingly important economic benefits. If either side considers that the conflict affects its vital interests, it can threaten to go to war and, in the end, actually call upon its military forces in a violent act of persuasion. At the point when the use of armed force is threatened, mobilized military capabilities become all-important, whether the readiness of the superior force settles the issue without actual fighting, or, if war actually breaks out, the arbitration takes place on the battlefield. In any calculation of perceived power it is essential, then, to expand our formula for calculating national power to include military capability: $P_p = C + E + M$.

To measure roughly the broad, quasi-psychological effects of power of the kind we are studying, I have adopted a weighting system for military capability that allows a maximum of 200 perceived power points, the same as for economic capability. A maximum of 100 points is allotted for effective nuclear deterrence based on nuclear war-fighting capability, and another maximum of 100 for conventional military strength. Most of the nations of the world will qualify only in the latter category. Obviously, these weighted elements of perceived power can be calculated only in gross, macrometric terms. Specific statistics are presented to anchor in detailed reality a highly subjective assessment of military capability as it is perceived as a useful instrument of national policy.

The most powerful weapons in the long history of war are universally considered to be nuclear bombs, artillery shells, demolition charges, and missile warheads, even though, except for their use at Hiroshima and Nagasaki in 1945, nuclear weapons remain untested under battle conditions. The overwhelming preponderance of Soviet and U.S. strategic nuclear strength is the dominant fact of international life. These two powers can literally extinguish the urban life of most other nations in a few moments, devastating it beyond recovery. Other nuclear powers pale into insignificance by comparision, but there is a certain aura about membership in the "nuclear club" that sets off the United Kingdom, France, the People's Republic of China, and now probably India and Israel from the rest. Even those nations like Japan, Sweden, Argentina, South Africa, Pakistan, and China/Taiwan that are widely perceived to have the technological capability to build nuclear weapons in a short period of months, enjoy among their neighbors a certain marginal advantage of respect or fear.

Nuclear weapons are so destructive that their capacity to deter other nations is their greatest military benefit. Except in an extremity hard to imagine (or in the event of unauthorized use), the United States and the USSR presently deter each other from nuclear war and seem likely to do so in the immediate future. Only if negligence in maintaining deterrent weapons makes one of these countries vulnerable to a crippling surprise first strike by the other, or if one of them achieves a secret technological breakthrough that neutralizes key weapons of the other, is war a winning proposition for anyone. Obviously, either of these nuclear giants can easily deter the secondary nuclear powers from using their much more limited arsenals.

It is, therefore, mainly the threat of the use of nuclear bombs or missiles – either as nuclear "blackmail" or nuclear "shield" – that brings enormous pressure to bear on normal international conflict situations. In a sense, the less responsible a nation's leadership, the greater the nuclear threat, for its use becomes more credible. Insofar as political leaders are moderate, and especially to the extent that they are accountable to public opinion, they can exploit nuclear capability as a deterrent rather than as a realistic threat. Yet without this ultimate strategic weapon, no nation today can pretend to be completely free to pursue an independent course in international affairs to the bitter end. Nonnuclear powers win contests of will on the sufferance of the USSR and the United States. In a true national life-or-death issue they would have to give way, unless they can secure U.S. and Soviet forebearance or unless the two superpowers neutralize each others' influence by supporting opposite sides in a struggle.

Fortunately, international conflicts are seldom pursued to the point of determining national survival or destruction. Such military action as has taken place since World War II has involved only conventional weapons. The era has not by any measure been a peaceful one, but no conflict has yet involved the actual employment of nuclear arms. The closest call was probably the Cuba missile crisis of October 1962, when the Soviet Union had a four-to-one inferiority in strategic weapons and delivery systems. Then U.S. superiority in conventional forces in the Caribbean pressed the USSR into a humiliating withdrawal of the medium-range missiles it had emplaced to bolster its limited intercontinental missile strength.

It is clear that in normal circumstances conventional military strength is the key to confrontations short of war. Conventional military strength also assures nations under attack from aggressive neighbors of some defense until the nuclear powers can contain the conflict and adjudicate or arbitrate it. Up to a certain point, a nation with effective conventional military forces can even defy the restraining influence of the nuclear powers and triumph over less well armed states. The takeover of South Vietnam, Kampuchea, and Laos by Communist conventional forces in the face of the efforts of the United States to prevent it is an eloquent demonstration of this point. The determining factor was in varying levels of national will. South Vietnam's armies were finally beaten on the battlefield with conventional weapons supplied by the USSR and the People's Republic of China while the United States stood by.

Crucial Elements of Military Power

Perceptions of military power are highly subjective, but it is clear that a weighting system for military capability has to take into account two elements. First, it may give primary importance to a persuasive and credible nuclear deterrence, whether total, as in the case of the USSR and the United States, limited, as in the case of the United Kingdom, France, and the People's Republic of China, or even marginal, as in the case of Israel and India. The perceived power of a nation is enhanced immeasurably if its nuclear-weapons strength is sufficient to face conventional challenges to the ultimate point before resorting to nuclear war. If a nation feared that its actual war-fighting capabilities in a nuclear exchange would prove greatly inferior, it could not even afford the risk of entering the struggle with conventional forces. Only the USSR and the United States can pass this test at present.

Since most future conflicts will probably be fought with conventional nonnuclear forces, a second element is the maintenance of respectable armies, navies, and air forces for general-purpose combat. While for the nuclear powers these conventional forces are probably of primary use only in confrontations of less than a national life-or-death kind, this is the way all military conflicts begin and the way all have been settled since World War II.

Conventional capability is doubly important because its use, or the threat of its use, guards the lower rungs of the ladder of escalation to nuclear warfare. A nation that can defend itself on even terms against a conventional thrust does not have to contemplate taking the awesome next step toward nuclear war. In this chapter only strategic nuclear forces are analyzed, the equally important assessment of conventional military forces being left for Chapter 6.

The Political Pressures Exerted by Nuclear Weapons

When national leaders are compelled to consider the strength of the strategic forces at their disposal, in a crisis severe enough to present the risk of nuclear conflict, the question uppermost in their minds must be the damage that their societies would suffer in the event of war. Moreover, even when the possibility of actual confict remains remote, as it will unless a nation's most vital interests are at stake, perceptions of each other's ultimate capabilities will limit the demands that national leaders feel free to make. It is impossible to forecast with confidence the interplay of move and countermove, but awareness of the risk of war, and a sense, however vague, of the ultimate balance of military strengths will act on people's minds and set tacit limits on their actions. In open societies public fears establish even greater limits on strategic options than a strict, well-informed analysis of the risks would warrant.

The limits on adversary actions set by direct nuclear deterrence are obvious enough. The leaders of the Soviet Union have not up until the present been able to order an all-out attack on North American cities without facing the unacceptable prospect that Soviet cities would in turn be destroyed. If this, indeed, were the only practical aspect of the strategic balance, we would scarcely need to bother to calculate the relative military capabilities of the United States and the

Soviet Union. No rational adversary would be likely to run the risk of provoking a full-scale nuclear attack on its own territory.

Deterrence depends upon the total balance of forces, however, and perceptions may be swayed by perceptions of the danger that diplomatic conflicts or actual military operations by conventional forces might escalate to a point where the possibility of a limited nuclear exchange becomes plausible. As Soviet strategic nuclear attack forces increase in numbers of warheads and accuracy, however, a threat of an attack on U.S. intercontinental ballistic missile (ICBM) forces might confer very great political leverage. If a Soviet capability to inflict the destruction of 90 percent of U.S. ICBMs in a single blow is credible, as strategic analysts all agree it will be in 1981 and 1982, the U.S. deterrent capability remaining would be limited to relatively inaccurate sea-launched ballistic missiles (SLBMs) and to slow, aging B-52 bombers in service since 1955. Moreover, in the past year it has been suggested that Soviet civil defense preparations might have reached the point of reducing Soviet casualties to about 10 percent of American levels in a nuclear exchange. These trends have roused worries that U.S. deterrence may be losing some of its credibility even now, and that American decision makers will be increasingly reluctant to enter into confrontations that conceivably could lead them to such an inequitable exchange.

Military planning must proceed on the basis of a possible surprise attack, however remote its likelihood. If strikeback forces are inadequate in any strategic setting, they will no longer serve to deter attacks in any conceivable circumstances.

It is the danger, therefore, that economic and political conflicts will escalate to the point where threats of nuclear war are implicit, and finally explicit, that American policymakers must think about and with which they must be prepared to deal. The political-psychological pressure exerted by the mere existence of nuclear weapons is the significant element in international power calculations. An implicit Soviet threat of a limited nuclear attack, coupled with readiness to put civil defense measures into effect, would put the United States under enormous psychological strain.

Looking ahead, the United States will undoubtedly continue to maintain a fairly reliable deterrent against direct nuclear attack, for two or three years. During this period, however, the Soviet Union will add some additional new capabilities, including a massive "counterforce" attack option employing its very heavy SS-18 ICBMs with ten multiple independently targeted reentry vehicles (MIRVs) each to destroy most of the fixed land-based missiles of the United States. This would leave Washington with the disheartening choice of firing its sea-launched missiles at Soviet cities, since they are not accurate enough to destroy remaining ICBMs in silos. This choice would be taken in the full knowledge that the USSR still had enough ICBMs left to kill 150 million Americans in our large, undefended cities. Well before this point is reached in actual military fact, the growing strength and effectiveness of nuclear forces in the Soviet Union can acquire a margin of perceived superiority in the eyes of political leaders all over the world. In the sense that the USSR will have more flexibility and more impunity in escalating conflicts to a high level of tension, this perception is already spreading. An image of superior strength enhances Soviet influence and prestige at the expense of the United States, and it tends to press the U.S. policymakers into strategic withdrawals and passivity. Inevitably, the effect in the long run will be to induce third parties to try to conciliate Soviet demands at the expense of U.S. interests or, if necessary, at some sacrifice of their own freedom of action. In the sense of giving the USSR a tacit veto over the policies of other states, particularly nearby ones, this situation is often described as "Finlandization"; the classical term is neutralization. Military capability, if it is visible and overwhelming, can force former adversaries into an impotent neutrality. Hence it is vital if the United States is to survive well into the 1980s that American nuclear weapons provide a credible deterrent at every step in a possible ladder of escalation toward a final nuclear showdown, not just the final, national suicide of total nuclear war. The military balance must be maintained at all of the crucial levels of threat and deterrent counterthreat.

Political judgments tend to be based on gross and unsophisticated perceptions. It is not the opinion of technical experts that matters most but rather the sometimes "unscientific" views of political leaders at home and abroad. Much of what follows deals with the factual aspects of the measurement of strategic power, but it should never be forgotten that perceptions are personal and judgmental, or that military strategy is politics, not simply a branch of engineering.

Trends in Nuclear Weapons Strength

The perceptions that would shape political evaluations and strategic plans during conflicts and potential escalation scenarios are not fixed; they are dynamic. A growing and innovative arsenal will be perceived as more powerful than one that is static — even if the latter still retains comparable advantages in purely technical terms. This is perfectly appropriate because political practitioners must always attempt to anticipate future power trends and not to base their policies on a static view of the present. The lead time for development and production of modern advanced weapons is from five to ten years. Hence it is prudent to note the trend line and rate of change along with absolute numbers as of the present. Here is where Soviet power has made great strides forward in the past decade.

A time graph showing numbers of the most accurate, destructive, visible, and highly advertised strategic weapon, the ICBM, reveals a rather startling reversal of comparative U.S.–Soviet numerical strengths over a twenty-year period.[24] (See Table 26.)

While the United States has not developed new strategic nuclear delivery systems since the mid-1960s, the USSR has produced an extraordinary array of new ICBMs. Their characteristics are summarized in Graphic II. The Soviet missiles deployed in the 1970s (the SS-17s, SS-18s, and SS-19s) replaced the older and less capable SS-9s and SS-11s. The SS-19 is considered one of the most important in the ICBM

Table 26. Intercontinental Ballistic Missiles (ICBMs)[25]

Year	United States	USSR
1960	18	35
1961	63	50
1962	294	75
1963	424	100
1964	635	200
1965	854	270
1966	904	300
1967	1,054	460
1968	1,054	800
1969	1,054	1,050
1970	1,054	1,300
1971	1,054	1,510
1972	1,054	1,550
1973	1,054	1,575
1974	1,054	1,590
1975	1,054	1,600
1976	1,054	1,550
1977	1,054	1,469
1978	1,054	1,400
1979	1,054[25]	1,398*

*The number of Soviet ICBMs has been reduced since the SALT I agreement in 1972 to permit an increase in sea-launched ballistic missiles (SLBMs) toward 950, the highest level permitted in SALT I.

force, and its MIRV tests have shown an accuracy of 0.1 nautical miles, or about 600 feet. Although little is known of the SS-16, reports indicate that about 100 are at present in storage, and they will eventually replace the SS-13s. The SS-20 is probably intended as a theater weapon, although it has the potential of being converted to an ICBM simply by adding the third stage of the SS-16. It would then reach targets in the United States.

It is impossible to state precisely how the political leaders of the United States or the USSR, or the leaders of lesser powers, will measure strategic strength in a crisis—certainly not by means of detailed numerical studies. More likely, people's views of the military balance are impressionistic, based on images mainly qualitative in nature. Thus bombers may be thought of as "old-fashioned" regardless of how effective

GRAPHIC II
U.S. and USSR ICBMs: Characteristics and Numbers Deployed, 1979[26]

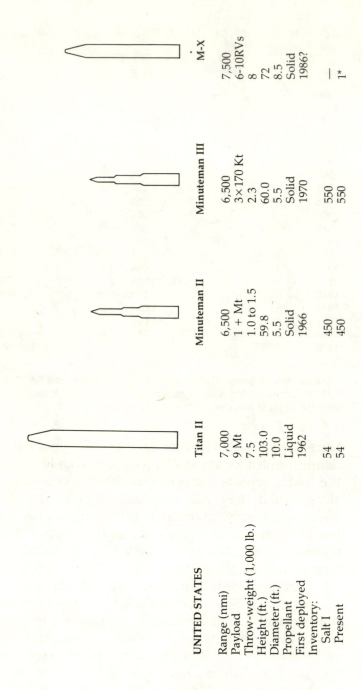

UNITED STATES	Titan II	Minuteman II	Minuteman III	M-X
Range (nmi)	7,000	6,500	6,500	7,500
Payload	9 Mt	1 + Mt	3×170 Kt	6–10RVs
Throw-weight (1,000 lb.)	7.5	1.0 to 1.5	2.3	8
Height (ft.)	103.0	59.8	60.0	72
Diameter (ft.)	10.0	5.5	5.5	8.5
Propellant	Liquid	Solid	Solid	Solid
First deployed	1962	1966	1970	1986?
Inventory:				
Salt I	54	450	550	—
Present	54	450	550	1*

USSR	SS-9	SS-18	SS-11	SS-17	SS-19	SS-13	SS-16	SS-20
Range (nmi)	7,500	7,500	6,500	5,500+	5,500+	5,000+	5,000+	1,900
Payload (Mt.)	1 to 25	15 to 25	1 to 2	5	5+	1	2	?
Throw-weight (1,000 lb.)	10 to 13	11 to 16	2	6	7.9	1	2	?
MIRVs		10	2	4 to 5	6		3 ?	3
Height (ft.)	110.0	120.0	64.0	70.0	80.0	65.0	65.0	50.0
Diameter (ft.)	10.0	10.0	8.0	7.5	8.5	6.0	6.5	6.5
Propellant	SL**	SL**	SL**	SL**	SL**	Solid	Solid	Solid
First deployed	1967	1975	1966	1975	1974	1969	1975	1977
Inventory:*** Present	100	208	630	150	250	60		

*The United States has a single M-X in the development stage; it will not be deployed for about five years. All U.S. production lines are closed down.

**SL = storable liquid.

***The Soviets have at least four follow-on ICBMs in deployment, and a fifth in development to be deployed in the early 1980s. Their total ICBMs in mid-1979 is 1,398; the U.S. total is 1,054.

they may be in the calculations of professional analysts, while weapons publicly and repeatedly described as "giant ICBMs" and "supermissiles" make a deep impression that far transcends any precise calculation of actual military usefulness.

Measuring Nuclear Capabilities

The clear-cut difference in the number of missiles allowed to the United States and USSR in the 1972 SALT I Interim Agreement and Protocol had a considerable psychological impact, while the countervailing factors such as accuracy of guidance systems, whose importance is so obvious to the professional experts, went almost unnoticed. After the signature of the accords, even casual readers of the daily press learned from constant repetition that the United States was allowed to deploy only 1,054 ICBMs compared to 1,618 for the Soviet Union. It was also clear that the maximum limits on SLBMs in SALT I were 710 for the United States and 950 for the Soviet Union if it was willing to take a couple of hundred of its old ICBMs out of its inventory, as it actually has done. Far fewer observers were aware of the substantial U.S. advantage in the number and combat quality of long-range bombers (approximately 400 B-52s versus approximately 200 TU-95s and M-4s), or in the number of separately deliverable nuclear warheads resulting from the 1972 American technological lead in adding MIRVs to its missiles.

Many nonexpert observers quickly concluded that the United States had conceded a certain position of strategic superiority to the Soviet Union, and that the SALT I accords were therefore a clear signal of a decline in U.S. strategic power across the board. While Soviet superiorities in SALT I were finite and contractual, the technological and qualitative advantages of the United States were usually perceived as a wasting asset, to be discounted in estimates of future power relationships. This perception has become more widespread as the USSR began adding MIRVs to its missiles, which are for the most part much larger than U.S. missiles and hence can carry more warheads.

The standard way of measuring the destructive effect of nuclear weapons is to calculate the equivalent force in conventional explosive material (TNT). This gives each weapon a yield of kilotons (thousands of tons of TNT) or megatons (millions of tons of TNT). In World War II the total of conventional bombs dropped by the U.S. Air Force amounted to only two megatons, the yield of one or two ordinary nuclear bombs today.

There is another useful measurement, the calculation of "throw-weight" or missile payload actually delivered over targets. Throw-weight figures tell us something useful, i.e., the ultimate potential capabilities of a strategic missile. Soviet missiles, and consequently their throw-weights, are mostly much larger than U.S. missiles. Thus in 1979 total Soviet throw-weight had reached the fantastic figure of 11.3 million pounds, whereas the U.S. total was 7.2 million pounds.

In a "city-busting" scenario, which lies at the heart of many early theories of strategic deterrence and certainly figures centrally in the popular imagination of nuclear war, the actual numbers of bombs or warheads that can be aimed at targets is very important. As people say, bombs and warheads are what hit you! The United States had more aircraft with bombs and small missiles aboard and more strategic missiles with multiple warheads in 1972, and it still outclasses the USSR in numbers of strategic weapons (bombs and warheads). The comfort that this area of superiority brings the United States diminishes as thick complexes of Soviet air defense make penetrations by aging U.S. B-52 bombers more costly in terms of attrition. Also the USSR is adding "MIRVed" warheads to its missiles at a rapid pace. The mid-1979 strength and composition of U.S. and Soviet strategic nuclear forces are indicated in Graphic III.

Because of the greater throw-weight of Soviet ICBMs and recent Soviet progress in "MIRVing" its missiles, the inventory of Soviet nuclear warheads is increasing rapidly and will reach a level of about 11,000 in 1982. The earlier start of the U.S. MIRV program has already given it most of its potential strength in numbers of warheads, assuming it observes SALT

106

GRAPHIC III
Composition of U.S. and Soviet Strategic Forces[27]
1979

MISSILE LAUNCHERS & HEAVY BOMBERS

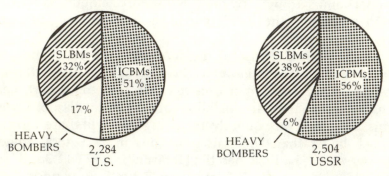

TOTAL WEAPONS

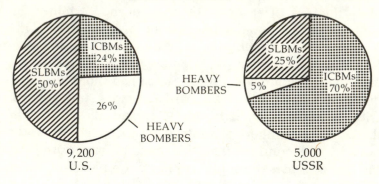

THROW-WEIGHT

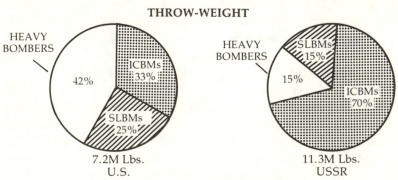

II limitations and does not MIRV its remaining single-warhead ICBMs. The introduction of cruise missiles after 1981 may increase the numbers of U.S. warheads somewhat. Therefore the total warhead strength of the two forces is likely to balance out sometime in 1982 at about 11,000 reentry vehicles for each nation.

Numbers of independently targetable weapons – what the U.S. Department of Defense calls "force-loadings" – make more sense to most political observers than the various technical calculations of megatonnage. It was the perception of substantial U.S. superiority in this category that made SALT I palatable in 1972. Perceptions of growing Soviet military capability in this respect, as in many others, have rendered SALT II to seem less tolerable. The history of the growth of U.S. and Soviet force-loadings is pictured in Graphic IV.

Even without major new discoveries, the energy yield extracted from every pound of payload has been steadily augmenting over the years as the technology of nuclear weapons has become increasingly refined. Similarly, accuracies have been improving as more refined guidance equipment is produced. Accuracy enormously improves the yield, the total destructive force exerted on target. In general, accuracies have been running at about 0.25 nautical miles CEP (circular error probable) and are now heading down to 0.10 nautical miles (about 600 feet). Eventually they will be almost pinpointed on target.

Given these technological changes, in the long run the measure of strategic capability will be set only by the capacity of the vehicles available to deliver payloads, that is, by throw-weight. This factor becomes especially important if numbers of launchers are limited by agreement (as in SALT I and SALT II) but numbers of missiles and warheads are not. In addition, this factor is complicated by the difficulty in precise verification.

As the USSR introduces increasing numbers of its three new multiple-warhead ballistic missiles into operational use, it will be working toward the ceilings prescribed in SALT II. At those high ceilings the USSR would increase its total throw-weight in its land-based ICBM forces alone from

108

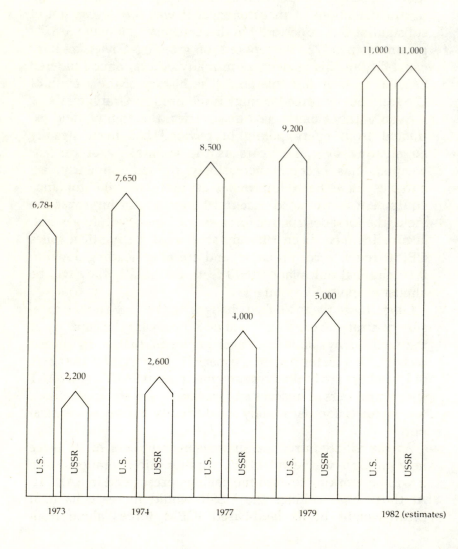

GRAPHIC IV
U.S.-USSR Strategic Nuclear Weapons[28]
(Bombs and Warheads)
("Force-Loadings")

almost 8 million pounds at present to about 10 million pounds by 1982. The throw-weight of the U.S. ICBM force is now only about 2.5 million pounds[29] and likely to stay there for at least five years, until a much larger missile than the *Minuteman* is deployed. This throw-weight advantage is a portent of future capability that substantially affects perceptions at the present time.

Overall missile throw-weights will measure actual capabilities only when the missile and nuclear technologies of both sides are equally advanced, and if the strategic arsenals are oriented to the same goals. At the moment the United States appears to enjoy a rapidly diminishing advantage in numbers of warheads, missile accuracies, booster efficiency, numbers of bombers, and "quietness" of SLBM submarines. In numbers of ICBMs and SLBMs, ICBM and SLBM throw-weight, numbers of SLBM submarines, and size of warheads, the USSR maintains a substantial superiority. When Soviet technology equals U.S. technology, as it is coming close to doing, the USSR will have the unique capability of firing over 300 very heavy missiles with as many as ten warheads per missile. This capability will create a situation in which many military planners will perceive a special U.S. vulnerability to a crippling first strike and thus in some respects a state of strategic weapons inferiority. This inferiority will probably become a reality about 1982 unless the United States initiates some countertrend.

Since the early 1960s, the United States has deliberately deployed forces optimized only for attacks on cities and other dispersed targets, as indicated by the very small warheads of the *Poseidon* submarine-launched missiles (40 kiloton) and the modestly sized (170 kiloton) warheads of newer ICBMs, the *Minuteman III*s. A new (MK-12A) warhead of approximately 400 kilotons is only now being produced for the *Minuteman*. The *Poseidon* and the present *Minuteman III* are not true counterforce weapons able to pin down Soviet missiles in a first strike.

The Soviet Union, on the other hand, has deployed some very large warheads (20–25 megaton nominal yield) on most of its "heavy" land-based missiles, and they clearly can carry a great many MIRVs. Under the SALT II Treaty provisions, the USSR is allowed 308 heavy missiles, whereas the United States is allowed none. The SS-18 has been tested with ten MIRVs. Thus when fully deployed the SS-18 force could have about 3,000 one-megaton warheads. A surprise attack employing only the SS-18s would be more than would be needed to destroy all of the U.S. land-based ICBMs.

It is this vulnerability of the *Minuteman* ICBM force that has troubled many American strategic planners and caused them to oppose SALT II, which freezes the Soviet advantage in heavy missiles and prohibits U.S. deployment of a similar weapon. The only candidate weapon system that can remedy this imbalance is the proposed mobile M-X, intended to be a missile large enough and accurate enough to be a counterforce weapon, i.e., to be able to destroy Soviet ICBMs. It cannot become operational before 1986 and is unlikely to be deployed in strength much before 1990.

This vulnerability of the U.S. ICBM force, compared with the relatively invulnerable Soviet ICBM strength, is the major reason why the USSR is widely perceived to be ahead of the United States in the strategic nuclear weapons balance. The U.S. weapons that might have redressed this imbalance — the M-X missiles, the sea-launched *Trident II*, and the B-1 manned bomber — have all been delayed or cancelled in recent years. These weapons deficiencies, plus the recent U.S. cancellation of plans for a new nuclear-powered supercarrier and the new theater-defense neutron bomb, make it necessary to rate U.S. perceived power in the strategic military category at least marginally inferior to that of the USSR.

Numbers of Strategic Weapons

A simple numerical summary of the array of U.S. and Soviet weapons systems and strategic-nuclear forces is presented in Table 27. The characteristics of the new Soviet missile types now being deployed are described in the first footnote to the table.

The United States, of course, will have no new missiles to

Table 27. Strategic Weapons Balance,*[30] mid-1979 (estimate)

Intercontinental Ballistic Missiles (ICBMs)	United States	USSR
Total ICBMs	1,054	1,398
Heavy ICBMs	0	308
Old Light ICBMs (U.S. *Titan* IIs)	54	0
Light ICBMs	1,000	1,090
ICBMs with MIRVs	550	608
Sea-Launched Ballistic Missiles (SLBMs)		
Total SLBMs	656	950
SLBMs on nuclear submarines	656	893
SLBMs on diesel submarines	0	57
SLBMs with MIRVs	496	144
Heavy Bombers**		
Heavy Bombers (Operational)	348	156
Total Operational Strategic Nuclear Delivery Vehicles:	2,058	2,504

*Heavy ICBMs for the USSR include the SS-9, and its replacement, the SS-18. The SS-19 is not classified as "heavy" under SALT guidelines. It is specified as the heaviest in launch-weight and throw-weight of the "light" missiles. It has a throw-weight of about 7,900 pounds, a little more than that of the U.S. ICBM, the old (1962) *Titan* II, that has a throw-weight of 7,500 pounds. The *Minuteman* II and III are much smaller. The USSR SS-17, with a throw-weight of 6,000 pounds, is included above in the "light" category. The others are the older SS-13 and SS-11.

**Heavy bombers include the U.S. B-52 and the USSR *Bear* and *Bison*. Thirty-five *Backfires* assigned to Soviet Naval Aviation are not included. The United States has 225 B-52s that are nonoperational.

deploy for some time. In addition to deploying a new fourth generation of missiles, the USSR is reported to have a fifth generation of missiles at various stages of research and development. The United States has a single new ICBM (M-X) in development and a single SLBM (*Trident*) in the earliest stage of deployment.

The United States and the Soviet Union also have other long-range delivery systems that are often regarded as non-strategic because they are qualitatively inferior or their performance is in some way limited. Soviet medium bombers can reach U.S. territory on one-way missions or on missions recovering in a third country such as Cuba. U.S. tactical strike aircraft deployed in Europe are capable of reaching the USSR, as well as Soviet long-range cruise missiles on board nuclear and nonnuclear submarines. The United States has a total of about 22,000 nuclear weapons. Of these 7,000 are deployed in West Europe, and many more are deployed at sea and at overseas military bases. Some 9,000 nuclear weapons are designated as strategic. For its part, the Soviet Union deploys a large (about 600) force of "intermediate" (IRBM) and "medium" (MRBM) range ballistic missiles targeted on West Europe and China; these antiquated weapons are now being replaced by the modern variable-range SS-20, capable of reaching anything in Europe or, in the Far East, anything in China or Japan.

Among the lesser nuclear powers, only France deploys a full "triad" of offensive forces; that is, intermediate ballistic missiles, sea-launched ballistic missiles, and short-range bomber forcers. The United Kingdom's only strategic force consists of four ballistic-missile submarines, although it has a few long-range bombers whose capability to penetrate Soviet territory is doubtful. The People's Republic of China has not yet deployed a submarine element in its strategic arsenal but has a modest force of medium bombers and is very slowly building a land-based missile force, presumably targeted on the Soviet Union. In addition, Chinese fighter-bombers capable of delivering nuclear weapons could reach Soviet and Indian targets. French and Chinese missiles are included as ICBMs in Graphic V because they can reach the USSR.

Defense Forces

There is an obvious imbalance between these vast offensive forces and the rather weak strategic defenses deployed on all sides, an imbalance that is historically unprecedented. In particular, there are no substantial missile defenses, prob-

GRAPHIC V
The Five Strategic Nuclear Powers*
1979

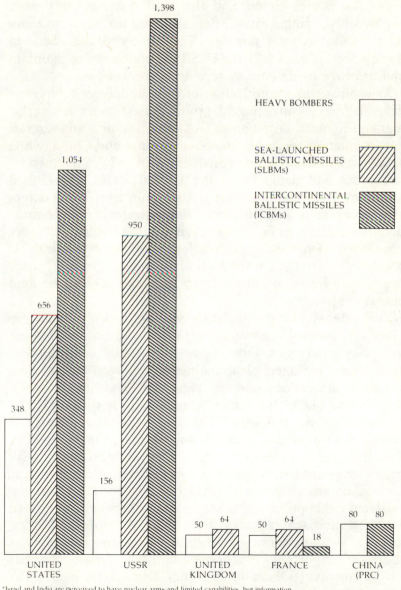

HEAVY BOMBERS

SEA-LAUNCHED
BALLISTIC MISSILES
(SLBMs)

INTERCONTINENTAL
BALLISTIC MISSILES
(ICBMs)

1,398

1,054

950

656

348

156

50 64   50 64   80 80
                    18

UNITED   USSR   UNITED   FRANCE   CHINA
STATES   KINGDOM   (PRC)

*Israel and India are perceived to have nuclear arms and limited capabilities, but information
concerning their strengths is too subjective for these countries to be included on this graph.

ably because the USSR and the United States both calculated that the costs were too massive. Such defenses would only spur both sides to deploy even more numbers of expensive and unneeded offensive missiles. Under the terms of the 1972 Anti-Ballistic Missile (ABM) Treaty, as amended in 1974, the Soviet Union and the United States may each deploy only a single missile-defense complex, with no more than 100 interceptor missiles. The United States chose to deploy none at all, while the USSR has continued to maintain and improve its defense system around Moscow.

As against this minimization of missile defenses, large air defense forces consisting of ground-based radar networks, manned fighters, anti-aircraft (AA) missiles, and anti-aircraft guns remain in service in the Soviet Union and China, while smaller air defense forces, consisting primarily of manned interceptors, are deployed in the United States, the United Kingdom, France, and in many other countries. These defensive forces make little difference in the strategic missile equation, particularly as far as the USSR and the United States are concerned. However, they do affect the category of strategic bombers where the United States is depending entirely upon the twenty-five-year-old B-52s so long as they can be kept operational.

The extensive anti-submarine warfare (ASW) forces deployed by the major powers constitute an additional element in strategic defenses, though one not usually designated as such. There is no technical distinction between tactical (i.e., shipping protection) and strategic ASW, although operationally the use of the forces would be quite different. The United Kingdom, the Soviet Union, and the United States all deploy nuclear-powered attack submarines, the most effective single ASW weapons, though by its very nature any ASW campaign would have to be a coordinated effort involving land-based search aircraft, surface warships, sea-based aircraft and helicopters, and seabed acoustic sensor grids as well as attack submarines. For the time being, the peculiar properties of seawater continue to limit the range and reliability of the most important detection equipment, sonar, in all its various forms. Ballistic-missile launching submarines, while by no means immune to attack, are relatively secure.

A final element in the nuclear equation is that of passive defense, the protecting of population, industrial capabilities, and military forces against nuclear attack. Since the deterrence of nuclear forces rests on the exorbitant cost of a retaliatory strike, the unequalled or unchallenged capability to limit the nuclear damage does affect the strategic balance. The U.S. civil defense program of the 1950s has for the most part been discontinued, a victim of a combination of costs, increasing USSR offensive strength thought to be beyond defense capabilities, and, at least partially, a general feeling that any nuclear war would be equivalent to Armageddon. The USSR has taken the opposite tack, devoting enormous efforts to the provision of personnel shelters, food storage, and protected industry. While there is little doubt that a U.S.–USSR nuclear exchange would be catastrophic for both sides, and while USSR passive defense capabilities may be exaggerated for psychological benefits, any substantial capability to reduce damage would necessarily become part of the decision-making process for both sides. If fully alerted and put into operation, Soviet civil defenses are calculated to reduce the damage from a U.S. second strike to something like 10 to 20 million casualties compared with 150 million American casualties from a Soviet strike on American cities.

Perceived Nuclear Power Capability

The strategic nuclear strengths of the United States and the USSR clearly overshadow the forces of all the other states, including those of the other nuclear powers. They possess at present a near-absolute deterrent capability and a roughly equivalent capability for waging a nuclear war in the event that one occurs. While the nuclear forces of the two superpowers are still approximately equal, there has been a change in the perception of relative nuclear strength. In recent years the USSR has closed a wide strategic gap and has reached parity with the United States. It has a dynamic and expensive missile development and deployment program and ongoing *Backfire*[31] bomber production, and is making extensive civil

Table 28. Strategic Nuclear Strength, 1978

Country	Perceived Power Weights
1. USSR	100
2. United States	95
3. United Kingdom	10
4. France	10
5. China (PRC)	10
6. Israel	5
7. India	5

defense efforts. In contrast the United States has cancelled its B-1 bomber program, the production of a new nuclear-powered aircraft carrier, and a neutron bomb for NATO. It has also failed to deploy new strategic missile systems. Increasingly, the USSR strategic system is viewed as innovative and aggressive, the U.S. strategic system as static and lacking in commitment. Accordingly, the strategic power weights assigned the USSR and the United States reflect this difference. They are mainly the result of the perceived trend line favoring the relative strength of the USSR over a period of many years. The trend can be reversed, but not unless the United States makes a substantially greater effort to build strategic nuclear weapons systems.

Both the United States and the USSR remain highly superior to other nuclear powers (Table 28). By comparison with the superpowers, China, the United Kingdom, and France have only minimal capabilities, sufficient perhaps to deter direct attacks by the major nuclear powers. In terms of nonsuperpowers, however, even their limited nuclear capability sets them apart regardless of the feasibility of the use of these weapons.

The United States, USSR, United Kingdom, France, and China all possess nuclear arms and the capabilities to deliver such arms; further, they acknowledge having these capabilities. There is a new and perhaps growing number of countries with much lower nuclear strength. They nonetheless are perceived as having nuclear arms and some limited delivery potential. For various reasons, primarily political, they are not likely to admit nuclear status, and our assessment necessarily becomes quite subjective. The two states of Israel and India fit this category. Their geographical placement and limited capabilities make it unlikely that they could threaten the major or even second-level powers, but this nuclear weapon status obviously changes regional relationships. Accordingly, Israel and India are included in assessing strategic force balance even though the primary effect is regional. South Africa has not been included in this examination for two reasons; first, there appears little substantial evidence that South Africa does indeed presently have nuclear weapons and delivery capabilities; second, the guerrilla nature of the war in South Africa fails to provide clear political or military targets for the use of such weapons.

CHAPTER SIX

Military Capability: The Conventional Force Balance

$$P_p = (C + E + M) \times (S + W)$$

The destructive power of nuclear bombs and warheads is immense, but for this very reason the military use of nuclear weapons is also highly circumscribed. Only in the most desperate circumstances could nuclear weapons be rationally employed, and it is therefore only in the most intense crises that strategic-nuclear forces can credibly serve as the tacit weapons of diplomacy.

Since 1945 none of the nuclear powers has found itself in a predicament that justified the employment of man's most awesome weapons. By now they are so numerous in U.S. and Soviet arsenals that the thought of a full exchange staggers the imagination. Although the popular sentiment is based on fear rather than accurate analysis of probable effects, it is common to speak of the possibility of destruction of all human life on earth.

While, therefore, there is no denying the tremendous psychological and political pressure exerted by nuclear powers, perceptions of military capability are equally affected by the implicit threat constituted by conventional, i.e., nonnuclear armed forces. Conventional forces have been entered into combat with some frequency in the past three decades. Both in Korea and Vietnam the United States felt constrained to use only its nonnuclear military power. In the Mideast several wars, large and small, have been fought between Arab and Israeli and between Arab and Arab. In South Asia, two Indo-Pakistani wars have changed the map of the subcontinent and brought forth the new state of Bangladesh. In Africa, most recently, military intervention by Cubans with Soviet arms has mainly determined the political fate of Angola and Ethiopia, and continues to pose a widespread threat to regional stability.

In all these instances war has been conducted in the classic manner, as the final sanction of political conflict, whether domestic or international or both. Since conventional non-nuclear forces can still be used in actual warfare, the perceived power of nations possessing such forces must reflect comparative capabilities to threaten local and limited war as a diplomatic instrument of policy on the international scene. Inherently flexible and thus usable in doses large and small in all manner of ways, nonnuclear capabilities directly translate into international power that is visible and tangible in everyday perceptions.

Standard estimates of conventional military power, based mainly on manpower figures, combat units, and equipment inventories, are notoriously unreliable. In formulating these estimates, units and weapons are laboriously counted and great efforts are made to obtain the raw data on which the statistics are based. By contrast, the "intangibles" of military power, such as troop skill and morale, the quality of military leadership, the coherence of operational strategies, the flexibility, mobility, and outreach of forces, and even political morale, cannot be counted and listed. Thus they tend to be ignored. These intangibles are of course very difficult to define, and cannot be evaluated by any fixed and objective criteria, but estimates of military power that exclude them for this reason are not merely inadequate but misleading. In the actual reality of war, the intangibles count for as much or more than the number of men or the quantity of equipment—and in the case of equipment its quality often counts for more than mere quantity. In the Vietnam conflict, as in all the Arab-Israeli wars, statistical estimates have been grossly misleading as indicators of employable military power.

A compilation of worldwide military statistics, although informative about the world we live in, is largely irrelevant to this survey of military power as it is perceived on the international scene. Most of the world's 162 independent states keep armed forces primarily to control their own populations. Never deployed in war, rarely exercised for combat in the field, and mainly equipped with light weapons, these armed units are in reality police forces. Their greatest utility is normally as tangible counters in domestic political contests over control of government posts of authority.

Some genuine military capability is of course still inherent in these forces, whatever their usual preoccupations, but in most cases such capabilities are limited to purely defensive operations in protection of national territory. Hence most of the world's armed forces are not instruments of international power, except insofar as they may negate the offensive forces of others.

Main Factors in Combat Capability

To evaluate actual combat capabilities, subjective judgments must inevitably be made if the intangibles are to be taken into account. I tackle this difficult task in this assessment by applying a series of "conversion" factors or coefficients to basic troop strengths in a way designed to translate the statistics of manpower and weapons into units of estimated military power which can be compared internationally.* The evaluation begins with gross manpower figures of all active military services and those paramilitary forces that

*I want to express my appreciation for the idea of this estimative procedure to Professor Edward N. Luttwak of Georgetown University, who worked out the model for it while assisting me in research on my 1974 assessment of military power.

are so organized and equipped that they may be used either to give significant support to, or to take the place of, the regular active forces. Perceived combat capabilities are calculated on the basis of an average conversion factor, made up of four distinct elements pertaining to quality of strength.

1. *Manpower Quality.* This factor obviously is not meant to represent the human worth of the men and women in the armed forces concerned but merely their operational effectiveness in war. This is primarily a function of troop training and unit morale (not national morale, which depends on the particular circumstances of each separate conflict), as well as of officer leadership. The latter, often of crucial importance, will reflect the sociology of the officer corps more than anything else. It is therefore a very inflexible constraint on military strength; weapons can be bought overnight and troops can be trained in a year or two, but it takes a good part of a lifetime in the right environment to school officers with reliable skills and motivation.

2. *Weapon Effectiveness.* This factor takes due account of the quantity and quality of the weapons deployed, but only in the context of the armed forces concerned. It therefore differs from weapon efficiency, which is a function of the mechanical capability of tanks, guns, ships, and aircraft. In the case of quite a few nations' armed forces, actual combat capabilities can decline when more sophisticated weapons are brought into service. For example, the wealthy but primitive oil-producing states of the Mideast are now in some cases equipping their men with weapons they do not know how to use at all, such as advanced fighter aircraft, complex tanks, and large warships. Had these states bought simpler weapons they could have achieved some immediate military capability. By contrast, some nations' combat units with advanced military skills are notoriously underequipped, a notable case being the Canadian air forces.

3. *Infrastructure and Logistic Support.* This third factor covers a very wide field, from the adequacy of radar surveillance and control systems to the provisions of aircraft shelters, and from the operation of repair units in the field to the adequacy of supply stocks. Most of the armed forces of

the world rely on imported weapons and supplies. Routine estimates of military power do not differentiate between weapons locally produced and those imported; nor do they separate local supplies of the "consumables" (e.g., ammunition) from those that are imported. Dependence on imports amounts to a major detraction from national military power unless stocks are inordinately high; even then, the amazingly rapid expenditure rates of modern war quickly deplete materiel as well as men. This fact was forcefully illustrated in the Arab-Israeli war of 1973. Hence the state that is more self-sufficient in the necessities of war must be counted as the more powerful, other things being equal. Nonindustrial infrastructures, from naval port installations to ground control systems for the command of combat aircraft, together with military communication systems, now absorb a great deal of military expenditure. Allowance for these must also be made under this heading.

4. *Organizational Quality*. The fourth and last conversion factor is intended to reflect the qualities of armed forces as bureaucratic organizations. They must be supervised (managerial efficiency); they must maintain at all times a certain level of capability available on call (readiness); they must make detailed step-by-step plans to implement their recognized missions (tactical planning); and they must be able to respond well to direction and adjust to new and changing situations in the heat of battle (command and control). A key ingredient in all of these is relevant combat experience, for war introduces realism in the life of large military organizations. In peacetime, realistic training has to serve as a substitute for the testing of the battlefield. Without this test, armed forces often tend to drift away from reality as they cultivate their own bureaucratic urges and perpetuate their own past traditions, including those no longer functional. War imposes the corrective discipline of real conflict and crisis on these organizational drives.

The application of these conversion factors yields the estimated units of perceived combat capability set forth for countries maintaining approximately 100,000 men under arms in Table 29. These general assessments mask a multitude of complicating factors, and the weighting is highly subjective and subject to argument.

Not the least of the problems is the doubtful accuracy of the basic figures themselves and the difficulty of comparing unlike weapon systems and dissimilar objectives. The approach here uses basic manpower figures from *The Military Balance 1978–1979* [The International Institute for Strategic Studies (IISS) London] for all nations except the United States and the USSR. With a few exceptions, perceived conventional military power is dependent on active military and combat-capable paramilitary forces (not including most internal security forces, construction troops, and peoples' militias, but including border guards). The force is the "standing army." In perceptions of threat of local and limited war, this image tends to dominate reactions.

In general, therefore, reserve forces are not included, but in a few specified cases reserves that receive annual training or have proved capable of rapid mobilization and combat capability are included for a more accurate assessment. The figures for South Africa and Israel reflect the prompt availability of effective reserve forces in nations that are on semi-alert status most of the time because of local hostility on their borders. For the People's Republic of China, the basic active duty military manpower strength of 4,325,000 is not adjusted, despite the existence of enormous numbers of poorly equipped reserves, i.e., the Armed Militia (7 million), the Urban Militia (several million), and the Ordinary and Basic Militia (75–100 million). Mexico and the Philippines have been included for a more accurate assessment of the regions in which they belong, since their forces are only marginally less than the minimum 100,000 baseline. Australia and its strategically inseparable neighbor, New Zealand, are included because they are the only sizable countries in the South Pacific and actually have comparatively substantial navies. Their armed forces are treated as if they were a single joint force, which is the way they would fight in a serious crisis in their own area of the world.

Comparisons of U.S. and Soviet military manpower levels are especially difficult. While U.S. figures are readily

Table 29. Nonnuclear Military Forces, 1978 (estimates of equivalent combat capabilities)

A. Warsaw Pact

	Manpower (in thousands)	Coefficients Showing Quality of Strength					Equivalent Units of Combat Capability
		Manpower Quality	Weapon Effectiveness	Infrastructure & Logistics	Organizational Quality	Coefficient Average	
1. USSR	4,335*	0.7	0.9	0.7	0.5	0.7	3,035
2. Poland	307	0.6	0.7	0.6	0.5	0.6	184
3. Germany (GDR)	249	0.8	0.8	0.6	0.7	0.7	174
4. Czechoslovakia	186	0.8	0.8	0.6	0.5	0.7	130
5. Rumania	181	0.5	0.6	0.6	0.4	0.5	91
6. Bulgaria	150	0.6	0.7	0.6	0.5	0.6	90
7. Hungary	114	0.8	0.7	0.6	0.5	0.7	80

Total manpower: 5,522,000   Total equivalent units of combat capability: 3,784

B. United States and NATO

	Manpower (in thousands)	Manpower Quality	Weapon Effectiveness	Infrastructure & Logistics	Organizational Quality	Coefficient Average	Equivalent Units of Combat Capability
1. United States	2,068	1	1	0.9	0.8	0.9	1,861
2. Germany (FRG)	490	1	0.9	0.9	0.7	0.9	441
3. France**	502	0.8	0.7	0.8	0.6	0.7	351
4. United Kingdom	313	1	0.8	0.8	0.7	0.8	250
5. Turkey	485	0.7	0.5	0.4	0.5	0.5	243
6. Italy	362	0.6	0.5	0.5	0.4	0.5	181
7. Greece	190	0.7	0.5	0.4	0.5	0.5	95

Table 29. (Cont.)

B. United States and NATO (cont.)

	Manpower (in thousands)	Manpower Quality	Weapon Effectiveness	Infrastructure & Logistics	Organizational Quality	Coefficient Average	Equivalent Units of Combat Capability
		Coefficients Showing Quality of Strength					
8. Netherlands	110	0.9	0.8	0.8	0.6	0.8	88
9. Belgium	87	0.9	0.8	0.8	0.6	0.8	70
10. Canada	80	0.9	0.6	0.6	0.7	0.7	56
11. Norway	39	0.9	0.8	0.6	0.6	0.7	27
12. Portugal	64	0.6	0.2	0.2	0.6	0.4	26
13. Denmark	34	0.8	0.6	0.4	0.4	0.6	20
Total manpower: 4,824,000					Total equivalent units of combat capability:		3,709

C. European Neutrals

	Manpower (in thousands)	Manpower Quality	Weapon Effectiveness	Infrastructure & Logistics	Organizational Quality	Coefficient Average	Equivalent Units of Combat Capability
1. Switzerland†	19	0.8	0.5	0.6	0.5	0.6	11
2. Sweden†	65	1	0.9	1	0.6	0.9	59
3. Spain†	315	0.7	0.5	0.5	0.4	0.5	158
4. Yugoslavia	267	0.7	0.5	0.5	0.4	0.5	134
Total manpower: 666					Total equivalent units of combat capability:		362

D. Latin America

	Manpower (in thousands)	Manpower Quality	Weapon Effectiveness	Infrastructure & Logistics	Organizational Quality	Coefficient Average	Equivalent Units of Combat Capability
1. Brazil	274	0.4	0.4	0.4	0.3	0.4	110

	Manpower						Equivalent units
2. Cuba	159	0.4	0.5	0.3	0.4	0.4	64
3. Argentina	133	0.4	0.4	0.4	0.3	0.4	53
4. Mexico	97	0.4	0.3	0.5	0.3	0.4	39
Total manpower:	663					Total equivalent units of combat capability:	266

E. Mideast and North Africa

	Manpower						Equivalent units
1. Israel	400††	0.9	0.8	0.8	1	0.9	360
2. Egypt	395	0.4	0.5	0.3	0.4	0.4	158
3. Syria	228	0.3	0.6	0.3	0.3	0.4	91
4. Iran	413	0.2	0.3	0.2	0.1	0.2	83
5. Iraq	212	0.2	0.5	0.2	0.2	0.3	64
Total manpower:	1,648					Total equivalent units of combat capability:	756

F. Sub-Saharan Africa

	Manpower						Equivalent units
1. South Africa	203††	0.6	0.7	0.6	0.5	0.6	122
2. Nigeria	231	0.1	0.1	0.1	0.2	0.1	23
3. Ethiopia	94	0.1	0.2	0.1	0.1	0.1	9
Total manpower:	528					Total equivalent units of combat capability:	154

G. Asia

	Manpower						Equivalent units
1. China (PRC)	4,325ф	0.4	0.2	0.2	0.3	0.3	1,298
2. Korea, South	642	0.6	0.4	0.6	0.6	0.6	385
3. India	1,096фф	0.2	0.4	0.3	0.4	0.3	329

Table 29. (Cont.)

G. Asia (cont)

| | Manpower (in thousands) | Coefficients Showing Quality of Strength | | | | | Equivalent Units of Combat Capability |
		Manpower Quality	Weapon Effectiveness	Infrastructure & Logistics	Organizational Quality	Coefficient Average	
4. Vietnam	615	0.5	0.4	0.3	0.9	0.5	308
5. China/Taiwan	474	0.6	0.5	0.6	0.6	0.6	285
6. Korea, North §	512	0.4	0.6	0.6	0.5	0.5	256
7. Japan	240	0.8	0.6	0.7	0.8	0.7	168
8. Pakistan	429	0.3	0.4	0.2	0.3	0.3	129
9. Thailand	212	0.3	0.3	0.2	0.3	0.3	64
10. Indonesia	247	0.2	0.1	0.2	0.2	0.2	49
11. Australia/New Zealand§§§	83	0.8	0.3	0.5	0.3	0.5	42
12. Afghanistan	110	0.2	0.2	0.1	0.1	0.2	22
13. Philippines	99	0.2	0.2	0.2	0.2	0.2	20
14. Burma	170	0.1	0.1	0.1	0.1	0.1	17

Total manpower: 9,254,000

Total equivalent units combat capability: 3,372

*See immediately preceding text and note. Does not include 6.8 million ready reservists.

**France withdrew from the North Atlantic Treaty Organization (NATO) in 1966, but is still a signatory of the North Atlantic Treaty. For all practical purposes its forces are a component of the North Atlantic Alliance military strength.

†Both countries have reserves of which 150,000 to 225,000 are annually recalled for refresher training. For this reason these nations are included in this table. Total reserves are, for Sweden, 750,000; Switzerland, 625,000. While these strong reserve systems add a great deal to the defensive capability of Sweden and Switzerland, both with a long tradition of neutrality in Europe's wars, they cannot be treated in terms of international power perceptions as equivalent to mobilized forces.

††Israel has a uniquely effective system of mobilizing strength within seventy-two hours. Its ready force is only 164,000. South Africa also can rapidly mobilize citizen force to fill cadre units. Its ready force is only 65,000.

ƒSee text on Chinese reserves.

ƒƒExcludes 200,000 reserves.

ƒƒƒAustralia and New Zealand are included because they are the only sizable countries in the South Pacific. Their armed forces are treated as if they were a single joint force in this assessment. The Australian armed forces actually total 70,057 and New Zealand 12,623. In a serious crisis in their own area, they would be perceived and probably would act as a joint force.

§In 1979 the U.S. government raised its estimate of North Korean military strength to over 600,000, approximately equal to that of South Korea. The more widely known IISS figure is retained here.

available, Soviet manpower figures are difficult to obtain and to assess. The USSR has approximately 4.4 million men on active military duty, and about 460,000 in combat-capable paramilitary forces. Among the uniformed regular forces of the USSR, however, there is a sizable segment whose occupational equivalents in the United States are civilians – construction troops, railroad troops, etc. This segment is called "uniformed civilians" by IISS, thus making a distinction that is useful as long as one realizes that they have had military training, are an organized and responsive element of the military, and have some direct military skills that their occupational counterparts in the United States do not have. The question is: How many uniformed civilians are there and how much military capability do they contribute? IISS specifies 750,000. On the other hand, John M. Collins, an authoritative American scholar of military affairs, mentions that 400,000 troops are not soldiers in every sense because they are "committed to construction projects, transportation, and part-time farm labor."[32] Other sources confirm that such a group exists but do not provide quantification. For the purposes of this evaluation, the effectiveness of the uniformed civilians is arbitrarily set at one-quarter that of normal troops, and the IISS figure of 750,000 is accepted. In total then, the Soviet military manpower figure is comprised of 3,687,000 active duty, 187,500 equivalent uniformed civilians, and 460,000 paramilitary – a total of 4,334,500 troop-equivalents.*

The Warsaw Pact, U.S., and NATO forces constitute the bulk of the conventional combat capability of the world. The neutral (or at least not formally allied) states of western and southern Europe are not major military powers. At least one, Spain, has the potential of becoming an important part of NATO, and Sweden has considerable military potential to defend itself. Similarly the armed forces of Latin America are

---

*For this ingenious solution of the Soviet troop strength I am indebted to Lieutenant Colonel Harry Wilson of the U.S. Air Force, who assisted me enormously in assembling data and suggesting format for this version of my world power assessment.

not major military threats in the global environment. However, Brazil and Argentina have special naval roles to play in
the South Atlantic. Cuba demonstrates how much trouble a
comparatively small nation can cause if its military forces
operate abroad under the control and protection of a power
like the Soviet Union.

In recent years, the military balance of the Mideast has
been a matter of international concern as local wars fought
for local reasons have had worldwide repercussions and
threatened to involve the United States and the USSR. Conventional estimates of military power have shown drastic
changes in the region over time with the vast inflow of
military equipment—notably accelerated since the last Arab-
Israeli war and the 1973 oil crisis. In fact, however, in this
equipment-rich area, it is the human and organizational factors that tend to determine real-life military capabilities, and
these are apt to change slowly over the years as one generation of trained military manpower replaces another. The war
in 1967 showed that Israel is a military power that would be
of world caliber if its demographic base were not so small;
the war in 1973 later revealed this fact. In addition Egypt is a
solid nation-state of sufficient military resilience to launch a
major assault and then pass the test of a battlefield defeat
without collapse.

Three substantial sub-Saharan powers are listed as the
strongest powers of a separate zone. Of the latter, South
Africa is clearly the predominant regional military power.
The tough, small armed forces (10,800) and paramilitary
units (8,000) of Zimbabwe-Rhodesia are closely associated
with the South Africans but are fully engaged in a vicious
guerrilla war and are not listed here. Nigeria, with its huge
population and oil wealth, has significant military potential,
although its present armed forces do not now reflect this
potential. If civilian government is successfully restored,
Nigeria will be perceived as a more effective military power.
Ethiopia, now engaged in warfare on two fronts, has marginal
military capabilities although it is presently receiving large
amounts of training, aid, and equipment from Cuba and the
USSR.

Since 1945, Asia has been the primary zone of world military conflict, although Africa and the Mideast have come to rival it in this respect in the 1970s. Nevertheless, in Asia a number of countries, notably Japan, with what is now the second largest economy in the world, have followed deliberate policies of restraint in developing their military power. China (PRC), India, and Pakistan, the three strongest military powers of the area, are also the poorest in per capita terms; in each case the cost to society of modern capital-intensive forces is inordinately high. This has not discouraged substantial armament expenditures in the past, and there is no reason to believe that societal poverty will prevent further military outlays in the future. Conflict in South Asia is an ever-present possibility.

Strategic Reach

Unlike economic power, or for that matter strategic-nuclear power, the capability of nonnuclear military forces wanes quite rapidly with distance from the place where combat strength is needed. Armed forces formidable for internal defense, such as those of Switzerland or the People's Republic of China, have very little capability even a short distance beyond national borders. Logistic infrastructure and built-in mobility are necessary attributes of military power and may absorb an important proportion of the total resources allocated to the armed forces. But logistics and mobility do not themselves define the quality of "strategic reach," the ability to "get there" promptly ready to fight. Strategic reach is a function of geographic position and the capacity for long-range projection of manpower and firepower.

Because its vast territory gives access to both Europe and Northeast Asia, the Soviet Union had a great deal of strategic reach even in the days when its airlift and sealift capabilities over long ranges were in fact very small. Its railroads could put its troops, tanks, and artillery where they might be needed all the way from Berlin to Vladivostok. Geographic formation of a country and its position on the earth's surface are critical elements in strategic reach. The other elements are the availability and capacities of the vehicles themselves — both sealift and airlift — that move combat units long distances overseas. In addition a whole complex of bases and forces allow such airlifted and sealifted forces to get to and be used in conflict situations. Thus in the American case a residual system of worldwide bases (much reduced from the 1960s but still vital), the carrier task forces of the U.S. Navy, the entire Marine Corps, and the largest airlift capacity in the world combine to provide a unique degree of strategic reach.

Even the United States, a great sea power with a long tradition of exceptional strategic mobility, including airlift, has severely limited capacity for delivering its military strength overseas on short notice. Outside Europe and Northeast Asia where major U.S. forces are already predeployed, the global strategic reach of the United States amounts to the ability to deliver relatively quickly up to one-and-a-third marine divisions, and up to two (smaller) air-delivered army divisions together with a commensurate amount of air power, but without the normal complement of armor. This is only a fraction of the total armed strength of the United States, but still very much more than any other countries, including the Soviet Union, could rapidly deliver overseas.

Moreover, the United States has a major "forcible entry" capability in its amphibious assault marine forces and its aircraft carriers, which can provide substantial air power over any coastal area of the world. Of course, even in the American case, a global strategic reach does not amount to global strategic access; there are already a good many places in Europe and Asia where even a four-carrier task force (300+ combat aircraft) cannot provide sufficient air power to suppress local air forces, and where even one-and-a-third marine divisions cannot be landed with any hope of consolidating a beachhead. Additionally, although the USSR does not possess an equivalent force projection capability, its growing navy does provide a worldwide "presence" and an increasing capability to deny or limit U.S. projection of its own forces at long distances from U.S. shores.

Of course strategic reach does not have to be global in order to give international political significance to nonnuclear military capabilities employed in a local contest. For countries in regions of global importance, such as West Europe, the Levant, or Northeast Asia, even a regional reach will count for a great deal in the arena of international politics. Hence, in computing the final estimates of international military power in Table 31, variables reflecting strategic reach are factored into the equation on the basis of politectonic positions as well as of mobility on the ground and especially at sea and in the air. The multiplier used here to convert combat capability into total conventional military capability is designed to give values that put the nation with the greatest reach—the United States—near the top of the scale. The Soviet Union, while it is developing a "blue water" navy and airborne forces, is still primarily a continental land power. Its strategic reach is still significantly less than that of the United States, calculated crudely at a factor of 5 to 3 as of the present, mainly because of the geographical separation of its fleets into four remote sea regions and because of the still vast superiority of U.S. nuclear-powered aircraft carriers. Limited reach is indicated by a multiplier of 0.02 compared with the Soviet and U.S. multipliers of 0.03 and 0.05 respectively. Negligible reach is indicated by a multiplier of 0.01.

This method of conversion makes conventional military capability equivalent to and comparable with strategic nuclear forces capability. The total of 200 perceived power weights for maximum military capabilities is the same as the maximum for economic elements of power.

Scale of Effort

An additional process of manipulating data reflecting perceptions of military strength is the addition of bonus weights to the perceived power of those few nations that devote exceptionally high percentages of GNP to military expenditures. This factor is only relevant to nations with comparatively large armies and amounts only to a maximum of

Table 30. Scale of Military Effort,[33] 1978

Country*	Percent of GNP	Perceived Power Weights
1. Israel	23	10
2. Egypt	21	10
3. Syria	17	8
4. Vietnam**	15	8
5. USSR	12	6
6. China (PRC)	10	5
7. Iraq	10	5
8. North Korea	10	5
9. China/Taiwan	8	4 ·

*Iran, formerly spending about 15 percent of its GNP, has allowed its military effort to slow down to a virtual standstill and no longer belongs in this group of nations.

**The Vietnam figure is spongy, but in view of Vietnam's invasion of Kampuchea (Cambodia) and border skirmishes with China (PRC), this probably is a minimum estimate.

10 perceived power weights in the scale of military capability established in this assessment. Yet large expenditures do impress observers, and nations with minimal levels of expenditure—such as Japan at less than 1 percent of GNP—are viewed as not carrying an appropriate share of defense burdens. Only Egypt and Israel rate at the top of the scale. The natural breakpoint below which no bonus credit ought to be given appears to be about 8 percent of GNP, and there are not many nations with considerable armed forces that are making this level of effort. Most nations spend less than 5 percent of GNP on military programs. For the first time since before the Korean war in the early 1950s, the U.S. effort sank below 5 percent in 1979. The countries given this special bonus weight are set forth in Table 30.

Total Military Capabilities

All of these factors can now be combined in a composite

Table 31. Total Military Capability Assessment, 1979
(nonnuclear)

Country	Equivalent Units of Combat Capability	Strategic Reach	Net Total	Strategic Military	Effort Bonus	Total Perceived Power Weights
1. USSR	3035	0.03	91	100	6	197
2. United States	1861	0.05	93	95	—	188
3. China (PRC)	1298	0.02	26	10	5	41
4. Israel	360	0.02	7	5	10	22
5. France	351	0.03	11	10	—	21
6. United Kingdom	250	0.03	8	10	—	18
7. Germany (FRG)	441	0.03	13	—	10	13
8. Egypt	158	0.02	3	—	4	13
9. China/Taiwan	285	0.03	8	—	8	12
10. Vietnam	308	0.01	3	—	5	11
11. Korea, North	256	0.02	5	—	8	10
12. Syria	91	0.02	2	—	—	10
13. India	329	0.01	3	5	—	8
14. Korea, South	385	0.02	8	—	—	8
15. Turkey	243	0.03	7	—	—	7
16. Iraq	64	0.03	2	—	5	7
17. Spain	158	0.03	5	—	—	5
18. Japan	168	0.03	5	—	—	5
19. Italy	181	0.03	5	—	—	5
20. Germany (GDR)	174	0.03	5	—	—	5
21. Czechoslovakia	130	0.03	4	—	—	4
22. Poland	184	0.02	4	—	—	4
23. South Africa	122	0.03	4	—	—	4

Country	Equivalent Units of Combat Capability	Strategic Reach	Net Total	Strategic Military	Effort Bonus	Total Perceived Power Weights
24. Yugoslavia	134	0.02	3	—	—	3
25. Brazil	110	0.03	3	—	—	3
26. Iran	83	0.02	2	—	—	2
27. Netherlands	88	0.02	2	—	—	2
28. Greece	95	0.02	2	—	—	2
29. Belgium–Luxembourg	70	0.03	2	—	—	2
30. Bulgaria	90	0.02	2	—	—	2
31. Cuba	64	0.03	2	—	—	2
32. Argentina	53	0.03	2	—	—	2
33. Australia/New Zealand	42	0.03	1	—	—	1
34. Hungary	80	0.01	1	—	—	1
35. Canada	56	0.02	1	—	—	1
36. Denmark	20	0.03	1	—	—	1
37. Norway	27	0.03	1	—	—	1
38. Portugal	26	0.03	1	—	—	1
39. Rumania	91	0.01	1	—	—	1
40. Pakistan	129	0.01	1	—	—	1
41. Indonesia	49	0.02	1	—	—	1
42. Thailand	64	0.01	1	—	—	1
43. Sweden	59	0.02	1	—	—	1
44. Switzerland	11	0.01	0			0
45. Mexico	39	0.01	0			0
46. Burma	17	0.01	0			0
47. Afghanistan	22	0.01	0			0
48. Phillippines	20	0.01	0			0
49. Nigeria	23	0.01	0			0
50. Ethiopia	9	0.01	0			0

Table 32. Consolidated Ranklist,
Critical Mass and Economic
and Military Capabilities,
1978
(perceived power weights)

Country	Critical Mass	Economic Capability	Military Capability	Total
1. United States	100	146	188	434
2. USSR	100	85	197	382
3. China (PRC)	75	23	41	139
4. Brazil	80	15	3	98
5. Canada	56	30	1	87
6. France	28	33	21	82
7. Japan	44	28	5	77
8. Germany (FRG)	30	34	13	77
9. Australia*	50	22	1	73
10. India	52	11	8	71
11. United Kingdom	29	21	18	68
12. Indonesia	56	4	1	61
13. Italy	29	14	5	48
14. Argentina	31	7	2	40
15. Spain	25	9	5	39
16. Vietnam	28	—	11	39
17. Egypt	25	—	13	38
18. South Africa	23	9	4	36
19. Turkey	26	3	7	36
20. Korea, South	20	5	8	33
21. Mexico	27	5	—	32
22. Iran	18	12	2	32
23. Philippines	27	3	—	30
24. Saudi Arabia	12	18	—	30
25. China/Taiwan	14	3	12	29
26. Nigeria	22	6	—	28
27. Bangladesh	27	1	—	28
28. Pakistan	25	2	1	28
29. Poland	14	10	4	28
30. Israel	—	1	22	23
31. Zaire	19	2	—	21
32. Norway	15	5	1	21
33. Algeria	17	3	—	20
34. Thailand	17	2	1	20
35. Chile	15	4	—	19
36. Netherlands	—	17	2	19
37. Sudan	18	—	—	18
38. Iraq	5	5	7	17
39. New Zealand*	15	1	—	16
40. Yugoslavia	10	3	3	16

Table 32. (Cont.)

Country	Critical Mass	Economic Capability	Military Capability	Total
41. Libya	10	5	—	15
42. Rumania	10	4	1	15
43. Denmark	10	4	1	15
44. Germany (GDR)	4	6	5	15
45. Korea, North	5	—	10	15
46. Syria	5	—	10	15
47. Ethiopia	14	—	—	14
48. Sweden	5	8	1	14
49. Czechoslovakia	4	6	4	14
50. Burma	13	—	—	13
51. Peru	11	2	—	13
52. Colombia	11	1	—	12
53. Venezuela	5	6	—	11
54. Morocco	10	—	—	10
55. Kenya	9	—	—	9
56. Tanzania	9	—	—	9
57. Mongolia	8	—	—	8
58. Finland	5	3	—	8
59. Belgium–Luxembourg	—	6	2	8
60. Greece	5	1	2	8
61. Zambia	5	2	—	7
62. Malaysia	5	2	—	7
63. Switzerland	—	7	—	7
64. Zimbabwe–Rhodesia	5	1	—	6
65. Guinea	5	1	—	6
66. Kuwait	—	6	—	6
67. Surinam	5	1	—	6
68. Bulgaria	—	3	2	5
69. Austria	—	4	—	4
70. United Arab Emirates	—	4	—	4
71. Hungary	—	3	1	4
72. Singapore	—	2	—	2
73. Liberia	—	2	—	2
74. Cuba	—	—	2	2
75. Jamaica	—	1	—	1
76. Albania	—	1	—	1
77. Portugal	—	—	1	1
			Total	2,745

*The military capability assigned to Australia and New Zealand in Table 31 is associated with Australia only in this table.

Table 33. Distribution of Perceived Power
by Politectonic Zones, 1978
(critical mass and economic and military capabilities)

Politectonic Zone	Country	Perceived Power Weights	Zonal Total
I	United States	434	
	Canada	87	
	Mexico	32	554
	Jamaica	1	
II	USSR	382	
	Poland	28	
	Rumania	15	
	Germany (GDR)	15	
	Czechoslovakia	14	
	Mongolia	8	474
	Bulgaria	5	
	Hungary	4	
	Cuba	2	
	Albania*	1	
III	China (PRC)	139	
	Vietnam	39	193
	North Korea	15	
IV	France	82	
	Germany (FRG)	77	
	United Kingdom	68	
	Italy	48	
	Spain	39	
	Norway	21	
	Netherlands	19	
	Yugoslavia*	16	
	Denmark	15	435
	Sweden**	14	
	Finland**	8	
	Belgium–Luxembourg	8	
	Greece	8	
	Switzerland**	7	
	Austria**	4	
	Portugal	1	
	Egypt	38	
	Turkey	36	
	Iran	32	

Table 33. (Cont.)

Politectonic Zone	Country	Perceived Power Weights	Zonal Total
V	Saudi Arabia	30	
	Israel	23	
	Algeria	20	
	Sudan	18	264
	Iraq	17	
	Libya	15	
	Syria	15	
	Morocco	10	
	Kuwait	6	
	United Arab Emirates	4	
VI	India	71	
	Bangladesh	28	127
	Pakistan	28	
VII	Indonesia	61	
	Philippines	30	
	Thailand	20	
	Burma	13	133
	Malaysia	7	
	Singapore	2	
VIII	Japan	77	
	Korea, South	33	139
	China/Taiwan	29	
IX	Brazil	98	
	Argentina	40	
	Chile	19	
	Peru	13	199
	Colombia	12	
	Venezuela	11	
	Surinam	6	
X	South Africa	36	
	Nigeria	28	
	Zaire	21	
	Ethiopia	14	
	Kenya	9	
	Tanzania	9	138
	Zambia	7	
	Zimbabwe–Rhodesia	6	
	Guinea	6	
	Liberia	2	

142

Table 33. (Cont.)

Politectonic Zone	Country	Perceived Power Weights	Zonal Total
XI	Australia New Zealand	73 16	89
	Total for all zones (77 nations)		2,745

*Communist but not aligned with either the USSR or PRC.

**Committed to neutrality. The total of perceived weights for the other countries of West Europe, all with close relations to the United States, is 386.

chart reflecting both strategic and conventional military power as perceived in international affairs, Table 31.

Zonal Summary of Concrete Elements of Power

With these adjustments, the assessment has covered the more concrete power elements of nations able to exert leverage in international affairs. The crude measurement it provides of these quantifiable factors in my formula is summarized, first nationally and then zonally, in Tables 32 and 33.

CHAPTER SEVEN

National Strategy and National Will

$$P_p = (C + E + M) \times (S + W)$$

All of the calculations reflected in the foregoing chapters provide a rough guide to the focal power weights in the world today. Most assessments stop at this point or well short of it. From the beginning, however, my strong conviction has been that only the foundation of a useful calculus of power has been laid down. The findings so far are still too simplistic, and they will be unrealistic unless the more concrete and quantifiable elements of power are modified by an estimate of two intangibles—the coherence of national strategy and the strength of national will.

These are the two most critical factors in my formula for measuring power. At the national level strategy (S) is the part of the political decision-making process that conceptualizes and establishes goals and objectives designed to protect and enhance national interests in the international environment. National will (W) is the degree of resolve that can be mobilized among the citizens of a nation in support of governmental decisions about defense and foreign policy. National will is the foundation upon which national strategy is formulated and carried through to success.

It is essential to note that the formula calls for a coefficient, i.e., a multiplier reflecting these two factors, S and W. While earlier elements of power have been treated as roughly additive, the use of a multiplication sign in the formula at this point means that the value of the whole equation can be substantially altered by the factors that constitute the coefficient for $S + W$. Thus, impressive concrete elements of power may be reduced to nearly nothing if a coherent national strategy is lacking or if there is little organized national political will to carry out whatever there is in the way of strategy.

As we now have rough quantifications for $C + E + M$, we can complete our assessment if we factor in the right coefficient to reflect the last part of the equation:

$$P_p = (C + E + M) \times (S + W)$$

Here we enter a region where numbers can only be notations of highly subjective judgments, nothing more. Yet the judgments are critical and must be made, even though reasonable men will inevitably differ on them. The task is simplified to some extent if it is recognized at the outset that most nations have only local or limited aims and are largely passive observers of strategic measures on a global scale. Powerful nations with broad international interests need and naturally tend to devise a global strategy to focus their energies. Secondary and tertiary powers fashion their national policies in accordance with the associations they have formed with more powerful nations. Most countries normally are preoccupied with either local or regional interests, but can summon up sufficient political and social cohesion to pursue their rather limited national purposes with reasonable effectiveness in the international arena if the need arises. Their national strategies are largely protective, i.e., defensive, and their national will is usually tested only in the relatively easy context of domestic self-defense. The alliances these nations join or the external influences they tolerate provide the best evidence of the coherence of their strategies and will.

In many cases, the coefficient will be 1, or normal, for combined strategic purpose (S) and national will (W); that is, 0.5

for strategy and 0.5 for will. If the multiplier is one, the value of the rest of the formula is unchanged. It is an arbitrary scale of measurement since most nations are perceived to have a limited impact on global power relationships or for that matter even on regional relationships, where their influence is more consequential but only decisive in the absence of superpower intervention in the region. This methodology permits focusing mainly on nations deviating above or below the expected behavior norm. By the standards of more concrete elements of power this fine tuning in the assessment affects nations perceived as major movers and shakers in the world arena.

In the case of nations with clear-cut strategic plans for international exercise of power and aggrandizement of influence, a larger index number for the factor S may be assigned, up to an arbitrary maximum of 1. If, similarly, nations are unified socially, psychologically, and politically behind strategic aims, they also may be assigned a larger index number for the factor W, up to an arbitrary maximum of 1. Thus a maximum score would result in a multiplier of 2 for the coefficient $(S + W)$. Other elements of national strength would be correspondingly magnified. In this way the total feasible score becomes twice the sum of the concrete elements of power previously summarized. The maximum total of 500 power weights that theoretically could have been assigned in recognition of the concrete elements of power, represented by $(C + E + M)$, could in theory now be increased to 1,000 although it is unlikely any real nation would have so high a score.

In fact, on the contrary, many nations fall below the normal level of 1 for their strategy and national will. In these cases, where nations are strategically confused and national will to pursue a policy is feeble, they may get a fractional index rating below 0.5 for one or for both of these more intangible factors. In that case the values for other elements of national power would be reduced. In an extreme hypothetical case, a zero multiplier for the sum of the intangible factors would give a zero quantity of perceived power, regardless of other potential strengths that may exist. A large and powerful nation with no strategy at all and no will whatsoever could hardly exist, but at various times even the greatest of nations suffer from an extraordinary confusion of strategic purpose and a comparable weakening of coherent national will. The history of U.S. foreign and defense policies in the past decade is a perfect example of enormous concrete elements of power rendered ineffective by muddled strategy and a lack of national cohesion. In the case of the United States the multiplier is less than 1, and that is the best proof of the validity of the formula in my calculus; there is no other way to reconcile the evident elements of concrete power with the worldwide perception of weakness and drift in American policy.

This calculation is critical in the whole analysis of perceptions of world power. In the exercise of great power, standards must be rigorous because the competition is severe. Hence any falling off by one of the large and potentially powerful nations, in these crucial matters of strategy and of strength of will, is a severe handicap in the use of power for international purposes. Factoring in these final, intangible elements of national strength therefore becomes the most important part of any net assessment of the international balance of power.

The final result of the application of this methodology is that the concrete elements of national power (population, territory, economic capability, and military capability) theoretically could be doubled or reduced nearly to zero, as the result of consideration of the less tangible qualities of strategic purpose and political will, for it is strategy and will that focus or dissipate the concrete elements.

Only three nations in the recent past have had an integrated, truly global strategic concept in the conduct of their international affairs. They are the USSR, the United States, and the People's Republic of China, all very large countries with tremendous strengths. Other nations for the most part orient themselves around—or against—these countries. They tend to form economic, political, and military combinations either with these three powers or with the four renascent secondary powers, Germany, Japan, the United Kingdom, and France. Regional associations of nations and groups dedicated to "nonalignment" with any of the great powers have also been formed, especially in Asia and Africa, but their exercise of influence in world affairs is limited. On the whole, the small and less powerful nations devote themselves in the international arena to propaganda and the weary wars of words at the United Nations. In the 1980s several newer nations of regional consequence, like Nigeria, Brazil, and Indonesia, are thrusting themselves into the ranks of globally involved powers, but in broad international strategy the number of major role players remains comparatively small and is likely to be so through the 1980s.

People join together in a nation because they share common purposes over and above their individual goals in life. Not everyone in a nation need agree on all those broader purposes, but there is a general direction or trend discernible in every community, whether or not it is clearly articulated. Most national goals concern such all-encompassing domestic issues as the distribution of wealth among citizens and the balance between authority and civil order on the one hand, and protection for individual and minority rights on the other.

In international affairs, the common purpose of a nation ought to include a general strategy for dealing with other nations in ways that protect and enhance the agreed goals of the citizenry, as represented by the government leaders entrusted with responsibility for foreign policy or, in any case, the leaders who have the power to make the decisions related to defense and foreign affairs. Though defense departments define military policies and foreign offices elaborate diplomatic positions, the bedrock foundations of foreign policy in a representative form of government must be the political aspirations and moral concepts of the people as expressed through their representatives at the national level. Strategy may sometimes be only a pattern of behavior rather dimly reflecting cultural norms; at other times, most especially in wartime, it is carefully articulated by the national leadership within the context of popularly approved values and goals.

In a dictatorship, policies can be worked out with precision and made mandatory. The range of possible international strategies runs from total isolation from the affairs of other nations (Japan in the early nineteenth century) to carefully plotted campaigns of territorial conquest (Germany under Hitler). In such dictatorial decision-making processes, public opinion is not consulted, only manipulated. Even when spelled out only vaguely in most citizens' minds, national policies determine the conditions for cooperation or conflict with other countries and hence, in extreme cases, the chances for political life or death – for national survival or extinction. Good, bad, or indifferent – crystal clear in reflection of national interests and goals, or fuzzy, even schizophrenic – national strategy is the central purposive element in every nation.

Decision Makers and National Strategies

In the interaction of the established modern states, whether they are Communist dictatorships, on the one hand, or pluralist representative nations, on the other, the most important strategists are the persons who control the political decision-making process at the highest level. They are the ones who make foreign policy cohesive and effective or weak and inadequate. Strategists in the Soviet Union, the People's Republic of China, and the United States, at the best of times, have developed a pattern of action that has been clear, justified by the values of their society, and in support of long-term goals. The leaders of smaller nations have usually been obliged to observe rather than to act, to advise rather than to determine, and eventually to fall in line with the decisions of these major states.

Soviet Strategy

Since 1917, when the Bolsheviks seized power, the Soviet Union has pursued its strategic goals under a unitary dictator who proceeded with a single concept to guide his conduct but with great tactical flexibility and rhetorical camouflage. He normally emerged from a power struggle within the upper ranks of a bureaucracy exercising a monopoloy of state power. As long as he kept the various bureaucratic elements of administrative and policy power in control, he held nearly complete authority in his own hands. He expected to try to advance Communist power to new heights domestically and into new territories externally, never doubting – at least publicly – that his aim was to establish a Marxist-Leninist system of government that eventually would spread across the whole globe. His time frame was not significant; the direction of his strategy movement was. A change of his broad objectives would put in question the very legitimacy of the regime.[34]

In 1919 Lenin described the classic world view of his generation of Communist leaders in the USSR: "We are living not merely in a state, but in a system of states and the existence of the Soviet Republic side by side with imperialist states for a long time is unthinkable. One or the other must triumph in the end."

For years Lenin's prediction of "frightful collisions" between the two systems was interpreted to mean that war is inevitable. After the terrible destructiveness of the hydrogen bomb sank home in the Malenkov-Khrushchev era, the doctrine was adjusted to say that war is not inevitable. Soviet military policy has always been built, however, on the premise that war may occur and that Soviet military forces ought to be able to win if they have to fight. The preferred strategy of the USSR is not a total war but the gradual political and economic undermining of the strength of leading capitalist nations.

Stalin made clear shortly before his death in 1953 the fundamentally economic character of basic Soviet strategy, predicting:

> It follows . . . that the sphere of exploitation of world resources by the major capitalist countries (USA, Britain, France) will not expand but contract, that the world market conditions will deteriorate for these countries and that the number of enterprises operating at less than capacity will multiply in these countries. It is this essentially which constitutes the aggravation of general crisis in the world capitalist system due to disintegration of the world market.

The USSR is still trying to see that the regions of the world where the international trading states get their resources continue to shrink as a result of the spread of Soviet control or influence.

Khrushchev, who became first among equals shortly after Stalin died, and assumed the office of premier in 1958, poured out from the mid-1950s a mighty flood of military assistance, along with a lesser amount of economic aid, to the countries the USSR hoped could be won away from cooperative economic and political relations with the United States and its "capitalist" allies. While not quite so generous or ebullient as Khrushchev, Brezhnev, who seized power from him in 1964, has continued to use arms and money to gain influence over peripheral areas and to try to separate them for the West. His aim is to control access to critical raw material resources like oil, gas, and rare minerals such as chrome, cobalt, and copper in the Mideast, Southern Africa, and Latin America.

Soviet advisers and Cuban troops threaten to cut Africa in two by exploiting Zimbabwe-Rhodesia's troubles and linking up the regions of Soviet influence in the African continent with similar strong points in Eurasia. Since 1975 the USSR has carried out a series of military interventions (usually with proxy Cuban troops in front of Soviet advisers and logisticians) in Angola, Shaba (Zaire), Ethiopia, South Yemen, and Afghanistan. The USSR has used its covert political intelligence assets and its formidable propaganda resources for less definitive indirect contributions to disorders in Iran. As these menacing moves have unfolded, the Soviets have brought about a major change in the patterns of stability in the area and jeopardized the access of the United States, West Europe, and Japan to the oil which is vital to their advanced industries as well as to their modern military forces.

It is no accident that Soviet-supported terrorism and guerrilla warfare break out wherever Western society is weak. Since the military occupation of Czechoslovakia in 1968 and the commitment to provide aid to the Palestine Liberation Organization (PLO) in 1969, Soviet practice has increasingly favored the kind of disorder that characterizes Iran today.

Despite disclaimers of responsibility, the Soviet Union has encouraged selected proxies like Cuba, Libya, South Yemen, and North Korea, as well as the PLO, to engage in guerrilla warfare and political terrorism.

Area by area, nation by nation, the Communist leaders have begun to make and predict they will go on making what the Russians call an "irreversible gain in the correlation of forces"—a decisive shift away from the United States and the West and toward the Communist bloc. Brezhnev explained on December 21, 1972, not long after President Richard Nixon's euphoric summit visit to Moscow, that the Communist party "still holds that the class struggle between the two systems—the capitalist and the socialist—in the economic, political and also, of course, the ideological spheres will continue. It cannot be otherwise, because the world outlook and class aims of socialism and capitalism are opposed and irreconcilable." And on February 24, 1976, at the 25th Communist Party Congress, he spoke triumphantly of Soviet successes in Vietnam and Angola and concluded, "capitalism is a society without a future." Furthermore, he said, "the international situation of the Soviet Union has never been more solid. We have entered the fourth decade of peace. Socialism's positions have grown stronger. Détente has become the leading trend. That is the main outcome of the party's international policy and the Soviet people can be proud of it."[35]

The Soviet world view has been consistent from Lenin's time down to the present day. In December 1978 Yuriy Arbatov, a member of the Politburo's Central Committee, defended the steady Soviet maritime expansion into all the world's oceans and especially into the Indian Ocean as natural under the "détente" policy. This policy was defined in early 1979 by political commentators in Moscow as "a special form of class struggle" that "rests on the shift in the correlation of forces in the world arena in favor of socialism." Soviet thought is clear about using all forms of Soviet power in supporting revolutionary class warfare against non-Communist governments and aiding what Moscow calls national wars of liberation.[36]

"Peaceful coexistence" in the Marxist-Leninist book (i.e., any concept of war the USSR favors to overthrow a non-Communist regime) in no way precludes policies or actions designed to achieve Soviet military, political, or economic predominance in any region. An international atmosphere of peaceful coexistence, which avoids the dangerous intensity of total war, tends to weaken the national will of non-Communist nations and furthers the expansionist aims of the USSR. If properly understood as the term has always been used in the USSR, peaceful coexistence positively calls for ideological warfare involving political subversion, guerrilla tactics, and national liberation wars—i.e., what I prefer to call a steady state of "coexistential conflict." In Soviet thinking, détente is the same as peaceful coexistence. It is the recipe for low-intensity war, an international trouble-making system that may benefit the USSR by installing new Communist or pro-Soviet regimes. It is almost certain to disrupt the economies and civil order of states cooperating with the United States and the other advanced industrial trading nations.

These concepts are taught throughout the USSR, and they constitute part of the furniture in the minds of those Soviet leaders in the Communist party bureaucracy who control foreign policy. Brezhnev and his most influential colleagues in the Soviet Politburo—Kirilenko, Kosygin, and Suslov—are in their seventies. Brezhnev himself is far from healthy and must certainly step down soon. His successor surely will come from a small group of bureaucratic loyalists nurtured in the same ideology. It is striking that Suslov, the paramount ideologue; Admiral Gorshkov, the father of the Soviet navy; Ustinov, the defense industry czar; Andropov, the head of the KGB; and Gromyko, the foreign policy expert, have all been in their jobs for more than a decade. Continuity and coherence are built into the Soviet strategy by the system. Some years hence, younger leaders may have different ideas, but for the present this national strategy of fundamental hostility to the non-Communist world and anticipation of recurrent resort to violence provide the best clue there is to Soviet behavior in international affairs. Détente is, and is likely to remain, a strategy by which the USSR makes itself safe from foreign threats, real and imaginary, while its leaders pursue revolutionary aims by other means. It is difficult to believe that the Soviets will accept any restraints in the form of arms control that would prevent them from ultimately gaining total strategic superiority over the United States. Soviet leaders know whose arms they hope SALT limitations will control; they expect to exploit the atmosphere of détente and arms control negotiations to inhibit American development of new munitions technology that might cancel out the gains in comparative military strength the USSR has achieved in the past decade.

The USSR now enjoys unprecedented power and prestige. It has grown in stature from an essentially continental power to a global superpower. Rivalry with the West will continue. Despite a degree of softness in their voices during the SALT II negotiations, the Soviets do not intend to cooperate more fully with the United States. They consider President Jimmy Carter indecisive, to say the least, and they will exploit his weaknesses. Soviet leaders brought up on Leninist-Stalinist ideology and conditioned by several decades of cold war with the United States will not fail to capitalize on such feebleness on the part of any nation.

Whatever current tactics might be at any moment, Soviet strategy toward the outside world is coherent and clear. It aims at accumulating power wherever and whenever prudence permits, and it assists in any movement that weakens states classified as enemies in traditional Leninist doctrine. Whether this strategy is ideological or nationalistic, or both, is irrelevant. It is an effective national strategy for improving Soviet standing in the world balance of power. It has the singular advantage that it is easier to tear apart the thin social fabrics of free civilizations than to construct them.

Chinese Communist Strategy

The existence of the People's Republic of China complicates every calculation made by decision makers in Moscow and Washington. In terms of national power China is not anything like an equal of the United States or the Soviet Union. As a nuclear military threat it is more in a league with

France and the United Kingdom. Nevertheless, China has throughout its long history always considered itself the ultimate central kingdom of the world, and as such, the greatest power on earth. Oriental patience and endurance are without limit. The Communists now in power have grafted this traditional cultural attitude onto Marxist-Leninist-Maoist dialectics.

The ultimate aim of the Chinese Communist party was pronounced by Mao Tse-tung and taught throughout China as infallible wisdom. The central elements of Mao's thought were collected in the famous "little red book" that was issued at the beginning of the Cultural Revolution of 1966–1968. It was waved by millions of "Red Guard" revolutionaries and recited by rote at countless meetings as the revealed truth for China and the world. While there has been a sharp falling away from ritual incantations of Mao's infallibility since his death, he is still the high priest—both the Lenin and the Stalin of the Chinese Communist party.

Mao's basic concepts were based on the emergence of the worker-peasant class at home and abroad and on constant revolution in the bureaucracies to maintain his own place as an idol of that class. In practical terms, he acted almost exclusively on the premise: "Every Communist must grasp the truth, 'political power grows out of the barrel of a gun'" (1938).[37]

His rhetoric about U.S. imperialists throughout most of his career was incendiary: "People of the world, unite and defeat the U.S. aggressors and all their running dogs! People of the world, be courageous, dare to fight, defy difficulties and advance wave upon wave. Then the whole world will belong to the people. Monsters of all kinds shall be destroyed." (1946)

The Chinese were still painting over wall slogans about "U.S. aggressors and all their running dogs" when President Richard Nixon arrived in Peking in 1972. At this time Mao turned toward the United States for protection from his bitter ideological rivals, the leaders of the USSR.

Before Mao's death in September 1976 the Chinese Communist leaders, under the guidance of their wisest propagandist, Chou En-lai, developed the strategic line of thinking followed to this day: "Countries want independence, nations want liberation, and the people want revolution. . . . There is a great disorder under heaven, [a state of affairs then described as] an excellent world situation." Many of Mao's theories have been retained by his successors although they have reevaluated some of his practices.

China's constitution adopted under Premier Hua Kuo-feng and approved unanimously on August 18, 1977, links the bright future of the "excellent world situation" with the Third World and explicitly rejects permanent coexistence with the USSR and the United States. It proclaims that the Chinese Communist party "unites with the proletariat, the oppressed people and nations of the world and fights shoulder to shoulder with them to oppose the hegemonism of the two superpowers, the Soviet Union and the United States, to overthrow imperialism, modern revisionism, and all reaction."[38]

There are serious doubts, however, as to how and when Communist China will be able to reach the ambitious goals it has set for itself. "We shall turn China into a powerful socialist country with modernized agriculture, industry, national defense, and science and technology by the end of the century," Premier Hua announced on the 29th anniversary of the founding of the People's Republic in 1978.[39] He followed earlier urgings along these lines by Chou En-lai and—after Chou's death—by his disciple, the oft-purged but durable Vice Premier Teng Hsiao-p'ing. Peking does not expect the four modernizations to materialize immediately, but it wants to make the Chinese Communist party appear to be the wave of the future, displacing present-day Soviet Communism as a model for revolution. When Vice Premier Teng came to Washington in January 1979 to formalize the establishment of full diplomatic relations with the United States, he obviously sought to bolster a sagging China with a vast Western economic and military aid program in direct defiance of the Soviet Union. Six months later his oratory emphasized the glorious tasks of developing an international united front against hegemonism in a world characterized by turbulence and tension. "Let us unite and march forward along the socialist road . . . under the banner of Marxism-Leninism—

Mao Tse-tung Thought."[40]

The decision makers in the PRC have formed a coalition government made up of leaders of the secret police, the state/party bureaucracy, and the military forces. Premier Hua won his office in October 1976 by a vote of one to nothing. The vote was cast by the only officer of the Standing Committee of the Politburo of the Communist Party, the elderly Marshal Yeh Chien-ying, left in office after the Gang of Four, including Mao's widow, were summarily arrested at Premier Hua's behest by secret security chief Wang Tung-hsing. Wang, a close friend of Hua, was later elevated to the top-level Standing Committee. Vice Premier Teng, chief of staff of the People's Liberation Army, from which he derives his strength, returned to an active role in the coalition. He had been twice toppled from power, once in 1966 and again in 1976, as insufficiently supportive of Mao's Cultural Revolution, and twice politically "reborn." The Peking regime is not a stable coalition, and China has no provision for its succession. Yet these leaders rule more than one billion people living in the heart of Asia.

As the present leaders see the outside world, China is beset with problems posed by the Soviet Union and the United States. In May 1979 the Chinese ambassador to the USSR accused the Moscow commanders of causing turmoil along their mutual border. He said, "They have carried out repeated intrusions to instigate armed clashes; they have stationed troops in Mongolia; they have deployed one million troops along the Chinese border."

Of quite another nature is the long-term problem of the Taiwan issue, which has created friction between the United States and the PRC for more than thirty years. This was brought to a head by the passage in the U.S. Congress in April 1979 of the Taiwan Relations Act (P.L. 96-8). Foreign Minister Huang Hua voiced his disapproval to the U.S. ambassador in Peking as the act was being discussed on Capitol Hill. He stated that it constituted a continued attempt on the part of the United States "to interfere in China's internal affairs. . . . This is of course unacceptable to the Chinese government."[41] Premier Hua is not inclined to let this issue rest, although the PRC has no military capability to do much about its goal of "liberating Taiwan" just now. In his formal report to the National People's Congress on June 18, 1979, he said in polite but firm tones, "We hope that the American side . . . will refrain from any action harmful to the return of China's territory, Taiwan, to the motherland, so that Sino-American relations will continuously progress in the direction that conforms to the wishes of both countries."[42]

The choices of action the PRC leaders have at present against the USSR or the United States are limited by poverty and overpopulation. However, they intend to expand their influence in the region whenever it is safe to do so. They vie for influence with North Korea against the predominant supplier of North Korean military weapons, the USSR. They initiated a limited war with Vietnam, and their substantial intervention in Cambodia in still going on. They intend, also within their capabilities, to expand their influence worldwide despite the slogan they propagate that "China will never seek hegemony or strive to become a superpower." The weakness and backwardness of their society is their biggest handicap. The PRC is a third-rate power with first-rank pretensions and a population problem that might well make it much less fearful of the casualties of limited and conventional war than any other state.

U.S. Strategy

In contrast with the strategic consistency of the leaders in the PRC and the USSR, decision makers in the United States since the mid-1960s have been moving steadily away from the policies that dominated the U.S. thinking about international affairs for the preceding quarter century. Policymaking in any nation under a system of representative government and multiparty elections is bound to be more diffuse than it is in totalitarian dictatorships where a comparatively small number of leaders are able to make secret and authoritative decisions. Moreover, much of U.S. policy is reactive, designed in response to situations created by other nations.

During most of its history U.S. leaders have avoided entangling international commitments, counting on the vigor of the nineteenth century British Empire to protect the Western Hemisphere from hostile intrusion. Despite a brief emergence into a wider theater in World War I, the United States clung to hemispheric isolation and neutrality with regard to international conflicts through the 1930s. There was a strong tendency to accept purely declaratory assurances like the Kellogg-Briand Pact of 1928, which renounced war as an "instrument of policy " but provided no sanctions to guarantee compliance. All of this ended abruptly in 1941 when Pearl Harbor vividly confirmed the argument of the interventionists of the period that the United States could not stay out of world conflicts but had instead an obligation to protect the interests of U.S. citizens abroad through positive action. In the "American Age" from 1947 to 1967 the concept of U.S. responsibility for security and freedom in every part of the world was the conventional wisdom of most political leaders and most American citizens. Presidents Harry S Truman, Dwight D. Eisenhower, and John F. Kennedy all had strong popular support in following a fairly coherent policy of "containment," i.e., firmly opposing by a variety of means all aggressive moves by Communist states against any and all independent nations that wished to be free to choose or maintain their own form of government. The Truman Doctrine and Kennedy's inaugural speech of 1961 evoked the spirit of the age of containment in its clearest terminology. Their strategy was based on a national commitment to defend a nontotalitarian way of life that would be endangered if the world power balance shifted decisively to the USSR or China, separately or collectively.

In the climate of confrontation and fractured consensus that followed the unsuccessful waging of limited conventional war in Vietnam, presidents Lyndon Johnson and Richard Nixon began to search for ways to ease tension between Moscow and Washington, increasingly accommodating to adverse changes, as in the final abandonment of South Vietnam and the victory of a pro-Soviet guerrilla faction in Angola. Suffice it to say, they promised too much in the name of "détente," and they left hazy in people's minds what the United States stood for unequivocally. It is hard to believe that U.S. leadership had become so enfeebled in comparison to the days of the Marshall Plan for the recovery of war-torn Europe in 1947, the dispatch of 8,000 U.S. troops from the 6th Fleet into Lebanon to stabilize the security situation in that nation in 1958, and the firm stance against the Soviet attempt in 1962 to place missiles in Cuba capable of destroying U.S. cities as far away as Washington.

In 1977, when the Carter administration came into office, our political and economic structure of international relations was as complex and challenging as it has ever been. However, the president's policies have never been developed, refined, or enunciated in a coherent way. The Carter hallmark has been vacillation and passivity in the face of international conflicts. The result has been confusion and inaction. In one of his first important public speeches at the University of Notre Dame in May 1977, President Jimmy Carter told the commencement audience, "First, we have reaffirmed America's commitment to human rights as a fundamental tenet of our foreign policy. . . . No common mystique of blood or soil unites us. What draws us together, perhaps more than anything else, is a belief in human freedom."[43] Yet, in his many negotiations with the USSR and the PRC he has never reproached these nations for their gross violations of all civilized standards of decency in the treatment of their own citizens.

In March 1978 at Wake Forest University, President Carter promised to maintain U.S. defense forces. "We are working on the M-X intercontinental missile and the *Trident II* submarine-launched missile to give us more options to respond to Soviet strategic deployments. If it becomes necessary," he continued, "to guarantee the clear invulnerability of our strategic deterrent, I shall not hesitate to take actions for full-scale development and deployment of these systems." Yet in the next few months he cancelled the B-1 bomber, delayed production of the neutron bomb, and slowed up work on the large mobile land-based M-X missile.

At the same time, while reviewing his thoughts about American strategic policy in general, he pointed out, "Japan and South Korea, closely linked with the United States, are located geographically where vital interests of great powers converge. It is imperative that Northeast Asia remain stable. We will maintain and even enhance our military strength in this area, improving our air strength and reducing our ground forces as the South Korean Army continues to modernize and to increase its own capabilities."[44] This pronouncement on the withdrawal of ground forces so upset the region that the president eventually had to reverse his policy decision and limit reductions in the strength of U.S. military units in South Korea to a relatively small number of those stationed along the heavily militarized North Korean border.

Again, in March 1979, at the Georgia Institute of Technology he lamented with what he called deep concern the eradication of the shah's government in Iran by the forces of the Ayatollah Khomeini and yet said, "We have not and we will not intervene in Iran."[45] President Carter's withdrawal to the sidelines of the world's geopolitical conflicts, after thirty years of U.S. support for stabilizing and economically modernizing regimes like the shah's, created immense alarm and a deep sense of instability in the whole Mideast area as well as in Africa. The loss of Iran is crucial to the industrialized nations of the entire world, not only to the United States, because their access to oil produced in the Persian Gulf region, which the shah's military forces had served to protect, is essential for their very existence as modern societies. Saudi Arabia and the other Persian Gulf states feel exposed. Iraq has become more ambivalent than before about its relations with the West, and more inclined to use its Soviet-supplied arms to increase its influence in the area. The rest of the Arab states, most of them hitherto fairly moderate in their policies and reasonably cooperative with the United States, have become restive. They feel vulnerable to Soviet clandestine political penetration and direct military pressure from Soviet-controlled Cuban proxy troops in Ethiopia and Yemen (Aden). President Carter's own peace talks with Anwar Sadat and Menachem Begin have yielded only limited agreements between Egypt and Israel; hope is waning for any early solution to the complicated issues dividing the Israelis and the

Arabs, and nearly all governments in the area are deeply mistrustful of the constancy and competence of the Carter administration. The longer the region is unsettled, the more opportunities the Soviet Union will have to improve its chances for injecting its influence throughout the Mideast from Afghanistan to Yemen (Aden) and on the African continent from Ethiopia to Mozambique and Angola.

The distinguished public servant, statesman, and diplomat George W. Ball, who served briefly as special adviser to the president on Iran, summed up the situation as follows:

> Unless we break out of our lethargy, we will face a dour day of reckoning. Then a violent argument will ensue as to why America so stupidly slept and reproaches and recriminations will defile the political dialogue. . . . The revolution in Iran requires us to re-examine certain key assumptions of our existing policy. . . . The repercussions on Saudi Arabia and other oil-producing states of our narrow focus on an Egyptian – Israeli treaty equally force us to question the methods by which we conduct that policy and specifically the current excessive indulgence in personal diplomacy.[46]

In our own hemisphere terrorism, guerrilla war, and forces of national liberation under Cuban and Soviet auspices have made inroads into Central America. They helped the Sandinistas gain power in Nicaragua and are working diligently with the guerrillas in El Salvador and Guatemala. The Cubans have an oversized embassy in Panama and have forged close links with radical regimes in Jamaica, Grenada, and some of the tiny islands of the Lesser Antilles. The Soviets have increased their representation in Mexico City and Costa Rica, in addition to building up their military forces in Cuba. After the Sandinistas overthrew President Somoza Debayle in Nicaragua to set up their own Marxist government, President Carter merely dismissed the event as an isolated happenstance. On July 25, 1979, he said, "It's a mistake for Americans to assume or to claim that every time an evolutionary change takes place or even an abrupt change takes place in this hemisphere that somehow it's a result of secret, massive Cuban intervention. . . . We have a good relationship with the new government. We hope to improve it."[47] The president simply ignored the fact that the Cubans themselves had admitted increasing support to the Sandinista rebels as the civil struggle intensified and that, in addition, the Soviets had deployed a powerful naval task force in the Caribbean on a cruising mission at the time Somoza fell.

The United States cannot afford much longer the strategic drifting and passivity of the past three years. We need leadership based on human decency, vigor, and experience in international problems. The 1980s will be a time of trouble, of crisis. The Chinese phrase for crisis, *wei chi*, is the combination of a word meaning "danger" and a word meaning "opportunity or power." The time of danger ahead is an opportunity for a U.S. leader to rise to the challenge and use the extraordinary, unique strength of the United States to solve problems and avert the perils that lie ahead. The experiences of the past forty years show him how to restore U.S. security, confidence, and pride in a world in which conflict and change is going to be constant. Yet, as of the latter part of 1979, U.S. strategy is schizophrenic and feeble, confusing to allies and U.S. citizens alike. It is impossible to rate U.S. strategic thinking as high as the norm that most major nations achieve, and it certainly falls below the Soviet level.

The Rest of the World

It is a reflection on the way global power is perceived in this era that we can turn from the three nations with pretensions to a broad, world-encompassing strategy to observe that the other 159 independent nations and about 2,862,000,000 people are pursuing regional strategies and trying to manipulate to advantage one way or another relationships with the USSR, the United States, and the People's Republic of China. The balance of power is changing from a period of U.S. dominance and is unstable. A few sudden key shifts could cause a movement of politectonic power clusters from one zone of influence to another.

In North America, Canada and Mexico have enjoyed reasonably close relations with the United States, but this is less true now than in the day of clearer articulation of U.S. strategy. At present, they both strongly stress political independence from the United States despite geographically determined economic and military interdependence. Anti-Yankee sentiment is not a substitute for a coherent strategy. Thus these two large and important U.S. neighbors add less to the power of North America than is suggested by their size and economic strength. Yet neither Mexico nor Canada perceives the need to increase its own military forces because of the feeling of protection afforded by the U.S. military deterrent shield.

Meanwhile, in the Caribbean, the influence of Cuba and hence of the USSR is growing. Castro's willingness to fight Soviet proxy wars in Africa and the Mideast means he can rely on a substantial Soviet military presence in Cuba and the Caribbean waters to guarantee his island against U.S. wrath while he overtly and covertly intervenes in political movements and revolutionary acts in Nicaragua, Jamaica, and Panama. Cuba has a clear strategy – to make trouble for the United States and governments friendly toward it.

Other countries in the Caribbean vary in the clarity of their aims and the solidity of their national will. The whole area will be unsettled and unsettling for neighboring North and South America throughout the early 1980s, at the least.

In East Europe, Poland and East Germany are subject to the political discipline of police states occupied by massive Soviet armies. Less regimented but equally under the Soviet heel, the rest of the Communist nations of the area follow the Soviet strategic lead. Rumania is no exception although it does so with ill-disguised reluctance. All are required to comply with the Soviet game plan in major matters without question. The power of these states is enhanced by a comparatively high coefficient for strategy, but the national will is comparably reduced. Public consent in the East European countries that are virtually occupied states most often lends fairly lethargic support to Soviet goals, and on occasion this support is very limited.

West Europe is not a strategic unity in any true sense, although each nation in NATO gains some degree of coherence in national strategy as a result of NATO collaboration and the leadership of the United States. The national will in these countries varies according to the domestic political situation. The United Kingdom articulates Atlantic goals effectively but is greatly reduced from its former levels of political and economic status. Germany, the state most closely identified with European U.S.–NATO strategy and the most politically disciplined, receives high marks for its national purpose. France is on a fairly steady strategic course of late, committed to the North Atlantic Treaty but insistent on playing its diplomatic cards independently. Italy skids along, always narrowly averting the troubles that full-scale Communist party participation in government would bring. Scandinavia and the Benelux complex play a useful role in NATO but, as small powers, tend to hedge against conflict with the USSR as much as possible. Both Spain and Yugoslavia are special cases, with reasonably clear strategies (to stay close to the United States and West Europe in the case of the former, and to stay nonaligned and independent in the case of the latter). In both of these nations, the domestic political situation is sufficiently unsettled to raise doubts about future political unity. Nevertheless, Spain is gaining political momentum because it seems to be creating a precedent proving that outside the Soviet sphere it is possible to make a transition from dictatorship to representaive (parliamentary) government. Portugal, although a NATO country, is in much the same transitional political state as Spain. Greece, torn by its antagonisms with a fellow NATO nation, Turkey, is in political difficulty both regionally and in its ties with West Europe and the United States.

In the remaining rimlands of Eurasia, the key countries from Turkey and Egypt around to Japan are all somewhat uncertain about their strategic future and about the degree of political consensus in their conduct of foreign affairs. Their aims are for the most part regional, local, or even tribal. Iran is probably the classic case of rapid political disintegration, but Pakistan is also shaky and uncertain about its future role. Afghanistan is virtually a Soviet-occupied state, although its tribesmen are resisting fiercely. India stumbles on in political turmoil with little policy except to be superior to other South Asian states.

Needless, to say, Sino-Soviet ideological and border conflicts continue to destabilize all of East Asia from North Korea down to the Indochina peninsula. The Asian nations taking the "capitalist road," as the PRC describes them in tones reflecting both condemnation and envy, are doing exceptionally well in recent years, from Japan, South Korea, and China/Taiwan to Indonesia.

Finally, the outer circle of states geographically more remote from the bipolar great-power conflicts continues to attempt to take advantage of this distance to pursue largely regional policies but with increasing difficulty in staying unentangled. These states differ enormously in their clarity of strategic purpose and internal political structure. Africa has clearly become embroiled in an astonishing array of contacts with the USSR and its surrogate, Cuba. Ethiopia embraces Soviet and Cuban military help to rebels in Zaire. South Africa makes desperate efforts to prevent revolutionary "liberation" wars from disrupting its economies and social systems. Nigeria and Kenya play a middle role in the spectrum of African political strategies, and Zimbabwe-Rhodesia is a test case as to whether the USSR can build on black-white tensions to intervene in guerrilla warfare that will leave it firmly ensconced in Central Africa.

South America, except for its varying reaction to Castro's Cuba, is simply a regional term for a group of nations focused mainly on domestic stability and economic growth. Brazil, Nigeria, and Australia of the outer circle are dynamic economically and psychologically, but at the present time their strategic and political ambitions are largely regional and even fairly parochial, like the bulk of their neighbors. South Africa has such serious domestic, social, and political problems that the defensive strategic positon that it is forced to take regionally and internationally severely inhibits the effective use of the considerable power it possesses. Yet, it has a clear, energetic strategy – of economic growth in the region as the key to political security.

Elements of National Will

Whatever strategy it may have adopted, and regardless of how coherent and clear its strategy is, a nation may be either efficient or inept in carrying out its policies, depending on the solidity of the political will of the people as expressed in their national decision making. National will may be unified and enthusiastic in support of a particular strategy or it may be sluggish and uncertain. The degree of energy and coherent behavior in a body politic is the main cause of its success or failure. Still, firmness of national will depends in part on whether strategic aims have been wisely formulated and skillfully explained in terms of national interests. This explanatory function is required in a representative government based on the consent of the governed. It is less so in dictatorships, but even in communist states consistent indoctrination is essential down the line of command. When the doctrine becomes unclear and the leadership divided, as in the PRC at the beginning of the 1980s, there is a falling off of effective national will just as marked as in a democratic state.

To have a defensible basis for quantifying the national will of the countries of the world, it is necessary to look closely at the identifiable elements that comprise nationhood: how people of a country perceive themselves in relation to each other as well as to the world around them, and how their society provides modes and procedures for acting upon those perceptions. These are the elements of national life that require analysis if we are to make sensible judgments about the phenomenon that my formula requires to be pinned down as a numerical coefficient.

National will is the quality that enables a nation to bring its resources and capabilities effectively to bear for a perceived national purpose, the nation's strategy. It is not a fixed quality; in fact it is ephemeral, fluctuating. The degree to which attitudes, values, and purposes are shared in a nation affects the strength of its will. Even more important is the character of the national leadership and, more particularly, the authority that leadership possesses to act, whether that authority has been bestowed by established tradition, popularly chosen government, or seized by force. No matter how achieved, the authority to act has limits and rests ultimately on the psychological reaction of the people toward both the leadership and the stated national strategy. Enthusiastic support is entirely different in its effect than sullen submission or passive resistance.

The elements of national will are multiple and diverse; no one element seems to be an absolute requisite for national strength of purpose. If a common language appears essential, then one looks to Switzerland, where multilingualism seems to be no impediment to unity. If ethnic uniformity appears to be vital, then one finds that great ethnic diversity had been largely surmounted and in a sense is a strengthening factor in the United States. Indeed, it seems that each nation offers a different combination of those individual elements that establish the degree of unity and strength of will that a nation possesses. Each case is separate and must be evaluated on its special merits or shortcomings.

Amidst this diversity, however, certain elements repeatedly emerge in contributory strands in the fabric of national will. These elements can be grouped as follows:

1. Level or degree of cultural integration of the people in a feeling of belonging to a nation;
2. Effective strength of national leadership;
3. Relevance of national strategy to national interests as they are perceived by the citizens.

Recent research on nationalism and the process of national integration has identified two factors as most significant: cultural uniformity and the concept of national territoriality.

The chief components of cultural uniformity are ethnicity, language, and religion. The degree of homogeneity in each determines the contribution each makes to national integration. Perfect uniformity is not required but the level of integration a nation achieves can be perceived in part—and measured—by the relative contribution of each component.

Where diversity exists, whether in plural ethnic backgrounds, multiple languages, or different religions, nations attempting to successfully integrate their populations make specific adjustments to accommodate this diversity, as Yugoslavia and Switzerland have done. Uniformity is not essential to nationhood in any of these powerful cultural factors, and each apparently can, in some cases, replace the other as a dominant force in integration. Another important component in the level or degree of national integration is the regard that the people have for their historical heritage, their collective memory of an often greatly idealized past. In almost every nation one can see a hearty, often even exaggerated, use of history as a binding force.

If the people who occupy a geographic area are to be fused into a nation, it is essential for those people to have a feeling of belonging and identification with a still larger or more abstract entity, their country. The stronger the psychological conviction is among the people that their own village takes its natural place on a national map, the greater will be the contribution this concept of territoriality makes to integration. If the citizens look outside their local environments to an unseen larger community of which they feel a part, they are on the path to nationhood.

In general, the longer a country has retained its essential geographic outline, the stronger the sense of territoriality becomes in the minds of its inhabitants. As the years become decades and the decades lengthen into centuries, people progressively regard the surrounding countryside as only an extension of their own homesteads. In some nations, however, the process of national integration has not been completed; it appears arrested by the greater prominence of, or greater loyalty accorded to, territorial entities within the nation. All countries of any size have a degree of regionalism, ethnic separatism, or tribalism; in some, it is strong enough to weaken the concept of national territoriality. This is most likely to be true when geographic regionalism is reinforced by cultural diversity, especially language or religion. The USSR, for example, has a special weakness in the great variety of national identities within its vast sweep of territory. The Great Russians who dominate Soviet decision making make up only half of the Soviet population, a large part of which is non-Slav and non-European—i.e., Turkic and Oriental ethnically, linguistically, and culturally. The differential birthrates favoring the population that is not Great Russian will cause increasing demographic strains in the USSR as the 1980s proceed. In most well-integrated nations the element of regionalism, ethnic separatism, and tribalism is subordinated to the national concept, especially when the nation confronts a substantial challenge. In much of Asia, most of Africa, and even in other areas, history and demographic evolution have left fragile and centripetal societies, some unlikely to last out the 1980s in their present national configuration.

To turn to another integrating factor in national will, the majority of the world's nations occupy geographic territory that is contiguous throughout and have within their national boundaries considerable uniformity of terrain and climate. Where the land is not contiguous, and where the geographic features are greatly dissimilar from one region to another, the concept of national territoriality is to some degree weakened. The people of Indonesia, who occupy an archipelago extending for 1,500 miles between the Indian and Pacific oceans, encounter greater difficulty in thinking of themselves as part of a single geographic whole than do the people of France. The people of Colombia, where part of the population lives in a temperate zone at a 7,000-foot altitude and where another part lives in a tropical climate at sea level, have similar difficulty. Increased communication and transportation networks, which result from industrialization, play a significant role in fostering national integration.

Because national will is ultimately the expression of the aggregate emotions and desires of a people, it is essentially a human response we are measuring, and human beings respond with greater intensity to some situations than to others. A national strategy evokes a level of response appropriate to the degree of national interest—that is, the aggregate of perceived individual interests—it appears to the populace to represent. Inevitably the highest level of such interest is evoked by a strategy perceived to be directed toward national survival. Examples abound of internally disparate societies rallying together during desperate crises. Other national strategies may be perceived by the population as considerably less closely related to the national interest, and they are therefore less likely to evoke a positive response. A strategy that seems to be concerned largely with aggrandizing the personal glory of the leadership, or that seeks mainly to elevate a minority group to a higher social or economic position, would clearly be less appealing to the populace as a whole.

In between these extremes lies an infinite variety of possible strategies. There are, to be sure, certain constants. Any national strategy that succeeds in enhancing the economic well-being of the majority of the population can be assured of some degree of positive response. Likewise, a strategy that seeks to achieve superiority over an established enemy, whether by economic competition or force of arms, can expect strong support from the people. Perhaps even broader response comes from a strategy of preventing a national enemy from achieving dominance over one's own country, at least if the danger of being outdistanced in the contest for power is clearly seen by the people as well as the leaders of a nation. Whatever the strategy chosen by the leadership, its perceived relevance to the aggregate interest of the people will be a significant factor in determining the response and support it receives.*

Final Ratings: Perceived Power of Major Nations

It is necessary to turn now to the task of quantifying the separate elements that together create the strength of a na-

---

*I am deeply indebted to Dr. Russell Jack Smith for undertaking the research and analysis that underlie the whole treatment of national will.

tion's will. This task is, if anything, more difficult and more subjective than the effort to quantify national strategies. Yet such an attempt can usefully illuminate the assessment, even though other observers may prefer to use different values.

In assigning weights to the various elements mentioned as contributing to the strength of a nation's will, it appears reasonable to give approximately equal weight to the three main groupings – national integration, strength of leadership, and relevance of strategy. My allocation of values within the three groupings, based on their relative importance in national will are then:

1. Level of national integration
   a. Cultural integration   25%
   b. Territorial integration   8%
2. Strength of national leadership
   a. Governmental policy capability   17%
   b. Level of social discipline   17%
3. Relevance of strategy to national interest   33%

It should be noted that the percentages suggested are for the several components of national will. In summing them up to total 100 percent I continue to work within an overall formula in which a coefficient or multiplier of 1 is the maximum rating, and a rating of 50 percent or 0.5 constitutes the normal or average. Few nations come even close to the maximum of 1, and many nations rate well below the norm of 0.5. Thus in our equation

$$P_p = (C + E + M) \times (S + W)$$

S and W combined result in a coefficient of 1 as the norm. More than 1 identifies exceptional clarity of strategy or strength of will; less than 1 indicates deficiencies in these characteristics.

Judgments about this final factor in the formula we have been using are bound to be mainly qualitative, rather than precise and quantitative; it would be unproductive to describe and defend in detail the coefficients assigned.

Prudence also suggests that no serious attempt be made to

rate most of the less powerful nations of the world for national strategy and national will. A few exceptions, however, are rather compelling. Some smaller powers with strong governments—whether democratic or totalitarian—and with clear national goals must be rated and ranked. Some, like Rumania, Cuba, Israel, Singapore, and New Zealand, take on a special significance because of their strategic locations linking them with larger countries. For example, Rumania, on the edge of the Soviet-dominated zone, is maneuvering for its independence; Cuba, in the U.S. zone of influence, is presently committed to the USSR; and Israel is virtually a U.S. outpost in a dangerous sea of Mideast states. Singapore is a key commercial entrepôt and—with Indonesia—a co-custodian of the Strait of Malacca; New Zealand is culturally and strategically tied to Australia and, to some extent, to the United States. All of these states must be assessed with care.

On the basis of the foregoing considerations, seventy-seven nations in all are assigned a coefficient for strategy and national will and ranked in the final assessment of comparative national power in Table 34 and zonal power in Table 35.

The striking fact emerging from these tables and from the entire method of analysis followed in this book is that national purpose and national will make a critical difference in the relative power of nations. The multiplication sign is the most meaningful part of the formula that constitutes my calculus of perceived power and strategic drift.

A totalitarian system has many shortcomings and its suppression of individual freedom and initiative cripples the development of a high level of achievement within a society. Nevertheless, the fact that the USSR has a coherent strategy and a tightly controlled population multiplies the brute power it projects into the international arena. The high rating shown in Table 34 derives from the efficiency of Soviet decision making and the discipline enforced on the Soviet people; it is diminished by the dulled responsivity of a population inured to dictatorship and by the decisive element of tension between Slav and non-Slav peoples.

The Chinese system has some of the same advantages, but it lacks a truly coherent national policy at this juncture,

Table 34. Consolidated Ranklist,
Final Assessment of Perceived Power, 1978

Country	Perceived Power Weights (C + E + M)	Coefficient			Total
		Strategy (S)	Will (W)	Strategy and Will (S + W)	
1. USSR	382	0.7	0.5	1.2	458
2. United States	434	0.3	0.4	0.7	304
3. Brazil	98	0.6	0.8	1.4	137
4. Germany (FRG)	77	0.7	0.8	1.5	116
5. Japan	77	0.6	0.8	1.4	108
6. Australia	73	0.5	0.7	1.2	88
7. China (PRC)	139	0.4	0.2	0.6	83
8. France	82	0.4	0.5	0.9	74
9. United Kingdom	68	0.5	0.5	1.0	68
10. Canada	87	0.3	0.4	0.7	61
11. Indonesia	61	0.5	0.4	0.9	55
12. China/Taiwan	29	0.8	0.9	1.7	49
13. Korea, South	33	0.7	0.7	1.4	46
14. Egypt	38	0.6	0.6	1.2	46
15. South Africa	36	0.7	0.4	1.1	40
16. Vietnam	39	0.8	0.2	1.0	39
17. Saudi Arabia	30	0.6	0.7	1.3	39
18. Israel	23	0.9	0.8	1.7	39
19. Spain	39	0.5	0.5	1.0	39
20. India	71	0.3	0.2	0.5	36
21. Italy	48	0.4	0.3	0.7	34
22. Argentina	40	0.5	0.3	0.8	32
23. Chile	19	0.6	0.7	1.3	25
24. Philippines	30	0.5	0.3	0.8	24
25. Netherlands	19	0.5	0.7	1.2	23
26. Pakistan	28	0.5	0.3	0.8	22
27. Nigeria	28	0.4	0.4	0.8	22
28. Mexico	32	0.3	0.4	0.7	22
29. Norway	21	0.4	0.6	1.0	21
30. Zaire	21	0.5	0.5	1.0	21
31. Korea, North	15	0.8	0.6	1.4	21
32. Algeria	20	0.5	0.5	1.0	20
33. Poland	28	0.5	0.2	0.7	20
34. Thailand	20	0.6	0.4	1.0	20
35. Turkey	36	0.2	0.3	0.5	18
36. Libya	15	0.6	0.6	1.2	18
37. New Zealand	16	0.5	0.6	1.1	18
38. Denmark	15	0.5	0.6	1.1	17
39. Germany (GDR)	15	0.8	0.3	1.1	17
40. Iran	32	0.2	0.3	0.5	16

Table 34. (Cont.)

Country	Perceived Power Weights (C + E + M)	Coefficient			
		Strategy (S)	Will (W)	Strategy and Will (S + W)	Total
41. Syria	15	0.5	0.5	1.0	15
42. Sweden	14	0.5	0.6	1.1	15
43. Rumania	15	0.6	0.4	1.0	15
44. Iraq	17	0.4	0.4	0.8	14
45. Peru	13	0.5	0.5	1.0	13
46. Yugoslavia	16	0.6	0.2	0.8	13
47. Sudan	18	0.4	0.3	0.7	13
48. Colombia	12	0.5	0.5	1.0	12
49. Bangladesh	28	0.2	0.2	0.4	11
50. Czechoslovakia	14	0.5	0.3	0.8	11
51. Switzerland	7	0.8	0.8	1.6	11
52. Morocco	10	0.5	0.5	1.0	10
53. Belgium–Luxembourg	8	0.6	0.5	1.1	9
54. Tanzania	9	0.5	0.5	1.0	9
55. Venezuela	11	0.4	0.4	0.8	9
56. Kenya	9	0.5	0.5	1.0	9
57. Zimbabwe–Rhodesia	6	0.7	0.5	1.2	7
58. Ethiopia	14	0.3	0.2	0.5	7
59. Greece	8	0.4	0.4	0.8	6
60. Finland	8	0.4	0.4	0.8	6
61. Zambia	7	0.4	0.3	0.7	5
62. Guinea	6	0.5	0.4	0.9	5
63. Austria	4	0.7	0.6	1.3	5
64. Bulgaria	5	0.5	0.4	0.9	5
65. Malaysia	7	0.4	0.3	0.7	5
66. Kuwait	6	0.5	0.3	0.8	5
67. Burma	13	0.2	0.1	0.3	4
68. Surinam	6	0.3	0.3	0.6	4
69. Hungary	4	0.5	0.3	0.8	3
70. Cuba	2	0.7	0.5	1.2	2
71. Mongolia	8	0.2	0.1	0.3	2
72. United Arab Emirates	4	0.3	0.2	0.5	2
73. Liberia	2	0.4	0.4	0.8	2
74. Singapore	2	0.6	0.5	1.1	2
75. Jamaica	1	0.5	0.5	1.0	1
76. Albania	1	0.5	0.5	1.0	1
77. Portugal	1	0.4	0.5	0.9	1

Perceived Power (C + E + M)   2,745

Total Perceived Power
(77 Nations) 2,625
(C + E + M) × (S + W)

Table 35. Distribution of Perceived Power
by Politectonic Zones, 1978
(final assessment)

Politectonic Zone	Country	Perceived Power Weights	Zonal Total
I	United States	304	
	Canada	61	
	Mexico	22	388
	Jamaica	1	
II	USSR	458	
	Poland	20	
	Germany (GDR)	17	
	Rumania	15	
	Czechoslovakia	11	
	Bulgaria	5	534
	Hungary	3	
	Mongolia	2	
	Cuba	2	
	Albania	1	
III	China (PRC)	83	
	Vietnam	39	143
	Korea, North	21	
IV	Germany (FRG)	116	
	France	74	
	United Kingdom	68	
	Spain	39	
	Italy	34	
	Netherlands	23	
	Norway	21	
	Denmark	17	
	Sweden	15	458
	Yugoslavia	13	
	Switzerland	11	
	Belgium–Luxembourg	9	
	Finland	6	
	Greece	6	
	Austria	5	
	Portugal	1	

Table 35. (Cont.)

Politectonic Zone	Country	Perceived Power Weights	Zonal Total
	Egypt	46	
	Saudi Arabia	39	
	Israel	39	
	Algeria	20	
	Libya	18	
	Turkey	18	
V	Iran	16	255
	Syria	15	
	Iraq	14	
	Sudan	13	
	Morocco	10	
	Kuwait	5	
	United Arab Emirates	2	
	India	36	
VI	Pakistan	22	69
	Bangladesh	11	
	Indonesia	55	
	Philippines	24	
VII	Thailand	20	110
	Malaysia	5	
	Burma	4	
	Singapore	2	
	Japan	108	
VIII	China/Taiwan	49	203
	Korea, South	46	
	Brazil	137	
	Argentina	32	
	Chile	25	
IX	Peru	13	232
	Colombia	12	
	Venezuela	9	
	Surinam	4	

Table 35. (Cont.)

Politectonic Zone	Country	Perceived Power Weights	Zonal Total
X	South Africa	40	
	Nigeria	22	
	Zaire	21	
	Tanzania	9	
	Kenya	9	127
	Ethiopia	7	
	Zimbabwe–Rhodesia	7	
	Zambia	5	
	Guinea	5	
	Liberia	2	
XI	Australia	88	106
	New Zealand	18	
	Total for all zones (77 nations)		2,625

despite its ambition, because Chinese leaders are jockeying for position in the struggle for power after Mao's death. The nation is not yet unified in pursuit of its long-range strategy and hence its coefficient for national will is low.

Clarity of national purpose and coherence of disciplined political will also show up in the ratings of countries like Germany (FRG), China/Taiwan, and Israel. The coefficients for the rest of the nations rated are derived from their current history, have a substantial margin of error, and reflect elements of human behavior that can change fairly rapidly.

National purpose and national will thus emerge as critical factors in determining power. The tremendous power potential of a country like the United States can be fully achieved only when its political leadership is unified and crystal clear in explaining national strategy and foreign policy. In these circumstances, as the highpoints of World War II and the late 1950s and early 1960s show, an open society with the support of the governed becomes virtually invincible in international affairs. At the end of the 1970s the American open society appears dispirited, vacillating, and weak.

The concrete elements of power $(C + E + M)$ total 2,745

perceived power weights for seventy-seven major nations. After multiplying by the coefficient for strategy and will (S + W), the perceived power weights are reduced to 2,625. In this final assessment the United States registers a 30 percent loss in contrast to a 20 percent gain for the USSR. The present correlation of forces, as Moscow would put it, or the balance of power, as Washington sees it, is delicately poised, but the direction of strategic drift is perceived to be toward growing Soviet political influence deriving from its military strength. This is so only because the United States, by far the strongest nation in the world in the concrete elements of power, has lost its psychological drive and is not playing the role of clear-sighted and steadfast leader of the Free World.

The final assessments reflect my judgment of the effectiveness of strategy and will of the nations that have considerable influence in the international arena. The equations in Tables 34 and 35 provide my scorecards for

$$P_p = (C + E + M) \times (S + W)$$

as we enter the perilous 1980s. Other observers may come to different conclusions and mark the cards accordingly. In any case these kinds of judgments about the main elements of national strengths and weaknesses provide the only realistic basis for calculating the balance of world power and formulating American defense and foreign policies to cope with the challenges ahead.

If this approach to rating individual nations for national strategy and will seems Olympian or magisterial, the only defense is to point out that it is impractical within the confines of this book to give each country the close political and sociological analysis it deserves. The coefficients listed in Table 34 reflect the author's personal evaluation based on long experience and extensive research in the field of foreign affairs and are only as good as the judgment behind the rating. This is plainly a game that any number can play; if readers disagree with the coefficient assigned, they can substitute their own and adjust the arithmetic or the reasoning reflected in this chapter. If the conceptual framework is valid, all reasonable men and women can write their own conclusions.

PART III

U.S. Grand Strategy and Foreign Policy for the 1980s

CHAPTER EIGHT

All-Oceans Alliance

The United States is facing the challenges of the last two decades of the twentieth century in a mood of anxiety and uncertainty over its rightful place in a rapidly changing world. In the mid-1970s the nation watched as very substantial pieces of territory in Southeast Asia and in Africa were taken over by totalitarian governments under strong Soviet influence, first South Vietnam, Laos, and Kampuchea (Cambodia), then Angola and Ethiopia. U.S. policy, after the bitter disillusionment about Vietnam, has appeared to opt for systematic withdrawal from strategic conflicts whenever they were costly, discarding allies one by one in the retreat if necessary.

The many nations that had in the past depended upon U.S. leadership in world affairs for their own security were shaken by the evident lack of firm U.S commitment in support of long-standing security guarantees. The complete withdrawal of U.S. forces from Vietnam, Kampuchea, Laos, and Thailand in Southeast Asia, and the Carter administration's blatant disregard in its first two years in office of the security interests of both South Korea and China/Taiwan in Northeast Asia sent shock waves through Japan and other traditional allies of the United States, even as far away as Israel and Iran.

In particular, the unilateral announcement in 1977 of the intent to withdraw U.S. ground forces from their blocking position along the demilitarized zone (DMZ) in South Korea

181

and the sudden decision in 1978 to terminate the 1954 Mutual Defense Treaty with the Republic of China created the impression that President Carter was anxious to escape military commitments to defend non-Communist countries that might actually fight to remain non-Communist. Rather than containing Communism, the president sought to avoid conflicts by establishing cordial relations with Peking, Pyongyang, Hanoi, and Havana, while continuing the pursuit of cooperative arrangements with Moscow in the spirit of "détente." He promised "a generation of peace," as Nixon had euphorically and unrealistically described it in 1972.

This policy of the Carter administration was notably unsuccessful, especially because it coupled encomiums to human rights with toleration of Soviet and PRC oppression at home and revolutionary violence abroad. It encouraged ideological enemies of the United States to more aggressive foreign moves, and confused, or drove to despair, American allies. There was a kind of naiveté and quasi-isolationism underlying this policy that is impractical in the interdependent world of today. Politics and economics no longer stop at the water's edge. Conflicts cannot be avoided by running away from foreign responsibilities. Walter Lippmann recognized this fact thirty years ago when he wrote: "American commitments and interests and ideals must be covered by our armaments, our strategic frontiers and our alliances."[48] If the United States is to survive, the nation must face global realities with a clear and coherent strategy, an adequate defense establishment, and a solid alliance system. Often these needs seem to be overlooked or erroneously taken for granted.

The course that holds most promise for the United States in the 1980s is a renewed emphasis on collective or mutual security with twenty or so key allies sharing economic, military, and political burdens. Perhaps it was too idealistic to try to contain the spread of communist governments at every point in the world, as presidents Truman, Eisenhower, and Kennedy suggested we should and could. Yet the United States must take the lead in preventing the communist nations, whenever opportunity arises, from gaining control of countries possessing the scarce economic resources upon which depend the prosperity and ultimately the political stability of the advanced industrial nations. Unless Americans can reinvigorate a worldwide alliance system, the United States will be gradually reduced to the status of an isolated Western Hemisphere power rather than a global power second to none. It is this latter vision that distresses most of the American people and most of the people in nations whose security interests and economic welfare are inextricably tied to what Washington thinks and does. The schizophrenic, vacillating actions of U.S. leaders in recent years have cast a shroud of gloom around the Free World.

What we need is a coherent foreign policy based on a strategy Americans and their friends can understand. I believe that U.S. strategy ought to focus on activating a series of informal, bilateral arrangements with nations interested in constituting a voluntary peacetime "All-Oceans Alliance." An association of seagoing, trading states could join together to provide mutual security against impingements on their freedom by any powerful, militarized despotism, whether Soviet, Chinese, Vietnamese, Korean, or Cuban. Such an alliance can ensure the protection of the collective national interests of open societies and representative governments if they commit themselves to a common strategic purpose with a full sense of the danger facing them.

From my viewpoint the model that persuades me to call for an All-Oceans Alliance is the fifth century B.C. Athenian League. Athens defeated the armies sent by Persian tyrants to conquer Greece, using not only its own resources and considerable sea power but also the voluntary fiscal contributions of other independent city-states, as well as ships and fighting men provided by its coalition partners. In this way the Athenian League created military forces more dynamic and better led than those of the much more powerful absolute monarchy the Greeks were fighting.

Nearly 2,500 years ago the Athenian League for a long time enjoyed remarkable success in keeping peace and protecting commerce in the whole eastern Mediterranean. The wellspring of what most Europeans and Americans consider civilization stems from this era. When the cooperating states later began to bicker among themselves over burden-sharing, Athens attempted to use naked force against its own allies to hold them together rather than working out common strategies. Finally Athenian politics and foreign policy became demagogic, and it was then that the alliance fell into disrepair. Ill-conceived and badly managed military ventures eventually destroyed it, finally bringing about the collapse of the fortunes and independence of all the member states.

If the United States could play the role of ancient Athens, and play it longer and more wisely, Washington would move to reconstitute a pattern of key alliances on the basis of common understanding of the problems ahead in the 1980s. Such an alliance must be strong enough to counter hostile moves by potential totalitarian adversaries. The ultimate aim is not imperial hegemony but a dedication to ensuring the safety and the political, economic, and social life desired by the nations' respective citizens. To evoke the best and most realistic aspirations of the people in each society is the real role of national strategy and ought to be the aim of U.S. foreign policy.

The U.S. alliance could espouse the essential purposes of the Atlantic Charter, including the security goals of the North Atlantic Treaty and the economic aims of the European community. It would have to be much broader, however, reflecting the global interests of the great trading states. It would embrace Pacific allies from Japan and South Korea in the Northwest Pacific to the ANZUS partners of the United States in the South Pacific—Australia and New Zealand. It would not replace any multilateral policy commitments and security guarantees derived from the great days of President Franklin D. Roosevelt, as well as presidents Truman and Eisenhower. It would restore their credibility, however, and broaden their scope geographically. Its functions would not be limited to military planning but instead would include economic policies and the sharing of information of common concern.

The central strategic task of the new, informal league of states would be cooperation to protect in peacetime or in war the sea-lanes linking the great trading nations of the Free World to one another. The area of operation would take in the three large oceans—the Atlantic, Pacific, and Indian—through which raw material resources move from suppliers to users. Membership in the All-Oceans Alliance would not require the signing of new agreements. There are already sufficient bilateral treaties between these ocean-linked nations. As a matter of policy, voluntary cooperative commitments and informal working agreements for naval and integrated land-based air patrols could be worked out by normal diplomacy.

Essentially what is called for is a strong guarantee of safe passage, either by sea or air, along all international routes, especially through the strategic chokepoints where blockade and harassment of traffic are potential hazards. What would be especially new would be extending the American security umbrella to the Indian Ocean and such key littoral states as chose, and were able, to fit into the All-Oceans system. Clearly allies would have to share the naval and air burden for collective protection of the new, enlarged territorial water zones. With their cooperation the United States could divide its forces into a Three-Ocean Navy, with supporting air forces, and maintain superiority at sea against any threat by keeping in the forefront of naval and air technology.

It is unrealistic to expect most of the less powerful nations to carry the burden or take the risks of performing as major participants in a global peacekeeping system. Many political, economic, and social changes will disrupt the power potential of the hundred-odd weaker states in the world today. Not all of them will survive, since local and tribal loyalties are strong and divisive in many regions.

The leading nations of the Free World, however, the core group of major international trading states, must stick together firmly in maintaining something close to the balance of power of the mid-1970s. Otherwise individual nations' losses of security and independence could accumulate and result in an irreparable shift of the balance of power toward the command economies of the totalitarian states. The tragic collapse of public order in Iran in 1978 and 1979 and the danger that pro-Soviet revolutionary groups will eventually gain control of this rich and strategically located state have brought home how quickly such shifts can take place in the absence of U.S. countervailing influence.

The strategy of building an All-Oceans Alliance for peace-keeping at sea will have a stabilizing effect politically in all regions. The combined power of the international trading states is more than ample to protect the peoples of friendly nontotalitarian states from bullying or outright aggression. Creating such an alliance is the only way to cope with U.S. global responsibilities in the short-of-war conflicts that are endemic in our times. It would permit us to put our national priorities in order and to rebuild the political consensus that will restore pride and self-confidence.

The policy of the alliance would not be the automatic all-inclusive "containment" of the 1950s and 1960s, but a new, conscious, positive program of economic nation-building and transoceanic cooperation with a select group of strategically important nations sharing the values of an open society or, at least, leaning in that direction as far as their circumstances permit. It would stress the constructive other side of containment that made it work for so long – the policy of building political and economic strength in the nontotalitarian world.

The main elements of newness in this strategy of collective nation-building lies in recognizing that all of the oceans of the world are one body of water and that the United States and its allies have to be able to command the seas to guarantee peaceful exchange of goods and services among free economies. This strategy also marks a new geopolitical awareness that the United States must protect its links with key allies not only in West Europe but in the Eurasian rimlands and outer circle regions of the globe. In short, the United States must provide safe passage through all the oceans of the globe. It has to take part in shaping the destinies of the nations scattered about in the politectonic zones that I have delineated in the earlier parts of this book.

Our main partners in international trade ought to help define and articulate on an urgent basis cooperative planning for an All-Oceans Alliance with an effective Three-Ocean Navy protected by adequate land-based air forces. The alliance must comprise, and only comprise, nations whose political systems are inherently compatible with ours, whose strategic positions make a difference in international power conflicts, and whose societies guarantee citizens' civil rights and leave a considerable degree of decision making in economic affairs to individuals as distinct from governments.

With these guidelines in mind, most Americans would easily agree that the member nations should include Canada, the United Kingdom, France, Germany (FRG), Italy, Japan, Australia, and New Zealand. I would definitely add Israel and China/Taiwan, two small but dynamic states counting on U.S. assistance to defend themselves against hostile, much larger neighboring countries. They are at the Mediterranean and West Pacific flanks of the alliance group and deserve to be included because they are cohesive and strong. Most of these nations are parliamentary democracies with closest political and cultural ties to the United States. For all these countries there is a residue of substantial popular support among the American people. Within the nations themselves there persists more willingness to believe in and rely on U.S. guarantees than in most other parts of the world.

Beyond this inner group of ten, we should not exclude a number of nations friendly to and anxious to be allied with the United States, whose individual economic or security problems, over which they do not have full control, hold them back from otherwise desirable guarantees of civil liberties and representative government. There are several states in this category that for strategic reasons must be brought into the core group if U.S. diplomacy and leadership are to rise to the task. They are Brazil, South Africa, Saudi Arabia, South Korea, and Indonesia, plus the mini-state, Singapore, which is inextricably linked with Indonesia in controlling the passageway between the Pacific and Indian oceans.

These are strong nations just now emerging into the status of influential regional powers. We should be leading them toward mutual security and political freedom in our alliance system, not coldly rejecting them as we sometimes appear to do. They need our help to prosper and grow in security, and we need their help to maintain a viable global association of seafaring states with a strong vested interest in international trade.

Finally, for a variety of strategic or economic reasons, an additional group of sizable nations would materially strengthen the alliance system if we could win and retain their confidence. They are Mexico, our populous southern neighbor; Spain and Turkey at the two gates to the Mediterranean; Egypt, a bellwether moderate Arab state; the Philippines, because of a long association with the United States and because it provides a major U.S. naval and air base in the West Pacific; and either Nigeria or Zaire, the two most populous and economically productive black African states.

Nigeria has by far the largest population in Africa and is comparatively prosperous because of its oil exports. However, it tends to be militantly dedicated to black rather than multiracial governance in Africa, a policy that is economically counterproductive and is politically contributory to conflict and tension with the only technologically advanced state in the zone, South Africa. Besides, Nigeria is not very cooperative with either the United States or the West European nations despite its extensive foreign trade.

Zaire is the eleventh largest country in the world and has the third largest population in central and southern Africa. Its difficulties arise from exercising government discipline over the many tribes and diverse provinces assembled into one state by Belgium in colonial times. Hostility on the part of the more militant pro-Soviet black states like Angola has also created economic problems for Zaire. The Mobutu government is cooperative with the United States, West Europe, and the more moderate African states, however, and Zaire is potentially capable of contributing to the stability, security, and prosperity of the international trading states.

While it would be good to have both Nigeria and Zaire as part of the All-Oceans Alliance, political forecasts indicate that in the near future Zaire is much more likely to be a willing partner in the cooperative arrangements envisioned. Its strength is therefore included, and Nigeria's is not, in my calculations of the potential power of a new voluntary association of trading states.

Ethiopia, the only other major country in the area, is certainly not a suitable candidate for a U.S.-led alliance system. If it continues for a few years longer on its present political course, Ethiopia will have to be considered part of the Soviet politectonic zone—an African nation wrenched from its regional affinities by Soviet influence, much like Cuba, already a part of the Soviet politectonic structure.

The All-Oceans Alliance I am suggesting includes at least one strong point in every non-Communist politectonic zone except in the subcontinent of South Asia. Ideally it should have at least one major ally in this zone. India and Pakistan are countries of consequence and would be suitable candidates if their internal political problems and their antagonisms toward each other should ameliorate enough to allow one or both of them to associate willingly with the Free World. India's links with the USSR and Pakistan's ties to the PRC complicate this process. In fact, the very existence of Pakistan is now in question because of the covert warfare in which it is involved in support of Pushtu tribes fighting against the Soviet-controlled regime in Afghanistan. This battle could go either way, and if the USSR persists and wins, the future of Pakistan's northern (Pushtu) area is not very promising. In short, the turmoil in the Indian subcontinent is so great that there is not much hope in the early 1980s, at least, for a constructive contribution to an All-Oceans Alliance from the southern Asian states. To win over India and Pakistan ought to be a U.S. foreign policy goal, but it would be reckless to count on either for some years to come. This fact makes a commanding naval presence in the Indian Ocean on behalf of the All-Ocean Alliance a first-priority need.

With any substantial group of these twenty-two nations tied to the United States and hence to one another across the sea-lanes of the world, an All-Oceans Alliance could act firmly and honorably to create an international environment safe for political diversity, orderly social change, nonviolent resolution of conflicts, and, above all, beneficial international exchange of goods. The key nations increasingly important in the world economy and to the United States are the advanced industrial states, especially Germany (FRG), the United Kingdom, France, and Italy in Europe; and Japan, South Korea, and China/Taiwan in East Asia. Their technology is the geopolitical prize of the 1980s. So long as they have access to the economic resources they need from across the oceans, these states alone can command enough military and economic strength to prevent successful Soviet geopolitical thrusts into any of the non-Communist areas vital to the stability and prosperity of the international trading system. Command of the sea on their behalf is the one area of military superiority within the context of broad strategic parity with the USSR that the United States cannot afford to relinquish.

Members of this alliance of trading states must learn to cooperate in formulating a policy that will weave together strands of mutually helpful military, political, and economic interest. Their economic links with one another and their political security must become part of a "going concern," to use Sir Halford Mackinder's phrase for an entity of geopolitical distinction. In his view a going concern has its own momentum, which is a great strategic asset. The dollars and cents of economic raw materials and international trade are simple enough to calculate. Threats to civil order, which are necessary for economic progress, ought to be seen as damaging to everyone, although some radical-chic political philosophers do not seem to be able to resist the romantic appeal of the Mao–Che Guevara type of revolutionist. Terrorist activities, including political strikes, sabotage, kidnapping, and assassination, simply cannot be allowed. The All-Oceans Alliance would be strong enough through collective efforts to stop these assaults on the fabric of civilized life in free societies if the threat is clearly recognized.

Above all, the United States must move to a strategy that is consciously global. The United States has trading partners in all areas of the inhabited world. Its trade routes fan out in every direction. They pass through the Caribbean and Panama Canal to serve both the east and west coasts of South America. They cross the North Atlantic to the United Kingdom, Scandinavia, and the Baltic, West European, Mediterranean, and Black Sea ports. Ships carrying Free World goods go from the Gulf of Mexico through the South Atlantic and Indian oceans to the Persian Gulf, and the Red Sea. From the west coast they cross the North and South Pacific to the Far East, putting in at harbors all the way from Japan down to Indonesia, Australia, and New Zealand.

The United States cannot afford to be divorced from its trading partners no matter how far they are from American shores. Except for Canada and Mexico, all of our trading partners are reached by sea. They, in turn, ship most of their commodities to the United States by sea. The shipping lanes even carry commerce via the Great Lakes waterways into and out of the very heart of the North American continent. Any prolonged interruption of seaborne commerce along these trade routes would be a disaster for the entire international trading community as well as for the United States. The nation's foreign trade alone amounts to about 13.7 percent of the world total, and is now equivalent to 16 percent of its GNP.

The much maligned country at the lower end of the African continent, the multiracial state of South Africa, holds a prime strategic position on the trade routes linking the Arabian Sea and the Indian Ocean with West Europe, East Asia, and the eastern seaboards of the Americas (see map, p. 192). The sea-lanes between Africa and the bruising currents and winds of Antarctica are narrow and dependent for navigational aid on the sophisticated ocean reconnaissance facilities and communications at the Cape of Good Hope. In any twenty-four-hour period about fifty-five ships loaded with oil from the Persian Gulf pass Cape Town. Iran, Saudi Arabia, Kuwait, Iraq, and the United Arab Emirates account for a large part of the exports of oil upon which West Europe and the United States depend. Ninety percent of the oil consumed by the NATO nations and 25 percent of what is consumed by the United States must sail through the Indian Ocean and around the Cape into the South Atlantic.

Most of the world's rare minerals by some geological accident are more plentiful in Sub-Saharan Africa than elsewhere. For this reason, and especially as a result of the tech-

Antarctica and the Southern Oceans

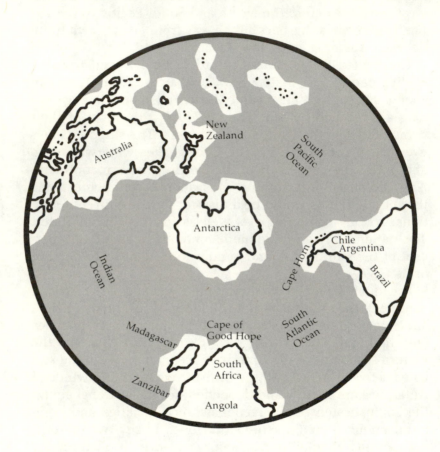

nological skills in mining developed in South Africa and to a lesser extent in Zaire and other neighboring states, this zone is the richest source of these supplies for the industrial nations. South Africa has, among many other minerals, gold, chromium, manganese, platinum, and uranium (in Namibia). Zaire has plentiful copper and cobalt; Zambia, copper; and Gabon, manganese. Only a few nations have supplementary supplies of the rare minerals. By far most of the world's exports of chromite come from South Africa, and most of the cobalt from Zaire. The United States must import 98 percent of its cobalt, 80 percent of its platinum, 99 percent of its manganese, and 91 percent of its chrome. The United Kingdom is in need of all these minerals, and it obtains 84 percent of its gold from South Africa.

Trade routes in the Pacific are no less important. Australia is very rich in mineral resources—it has approximately 20 percent of the known, easily mined uranium in non-Communist countries and is an important producer of lead, zinc, manganese, tin, nickel, silver, coal, and phosphates. Australia's greatest natural raw material wealth, especially in energy resources, is in the northern and western parts of the country. This places a premium on maintaining the security of the passageways connecting the Indian Ocean, Southeast Asia, and the West Pacific. Australian minerals are absolutely essential to Japanese industry. Japan imports nearly all of the oil its advanced technology requires in very great quantities, about 90 percent of it from the Persian Gulf and most of the rest from the Indonesian region. All of this oil travels by the sea-lanes of the Indian Ocean and through the Indonesian straits. The trade routes running to and from Japan and Korea via China/Taiwan and the Philippines and on into the Indian Ocean are becoming as vital to Free World trade as the Atlantic passages.

Australia and New Zealand, because of their isolated geographic location, are well aware of the value of foreign trade. Both countries have a continuing and growing interest in expanding commerce with South American countries, particularly those on the Pacific rim, with the main bulk in agricultural products. For example, they are making significant contributions to livestock improvement and pastoral development projects in various Latin American countries.

At a time of increasing world food and fuel shortages the South Pacific is a vital part of the food chain that makes ocean fishing profitable. The protein-rich krill (a Norwegian term meaning "tiny fish") teeming in southern waters and the potential energy resources of Antarctica are attracting the interest of many seafaring nations. The relations of South America and New Zealand to the icy continent is something to be considered in the light of possible future trading patterns in the South Pacific and Indian Ocean seafaring context. An All-Oceans Alliance is imperative if fish, fuel, and other minerals, such as the manganese nodules of the Pacific, are to be exploited safely and efficiently.

The hallmark of an All-Oceans Alliance would be a firm strategic commitment by the United States to defend the freedom of all the member nations who participate in international trade. Détente in the literal sense of taking every reasonable step to avoid war would, of course, continue to be sought by everyone. The leaders of the United States should, however, plainly recognize and explain to the American people that short-of-war conflicts over economic resources in the rimlands of Eurasia are likely to continue so long as governments in Moscow and Peking sponsor revolution, class warfare, and guerrilla liberation movements in other nations, and consider these conflicts compatible with détente. In other words, political leaders must find the courage to tell their people that, as Soviet ideology makes crystal clear, détente equals peaceful coexistence, which in Soviet propaganda means "coexistential conflict" or low-intensity warfare. This is the strategic situation now. The ups and downs in diplomatic atmospherics over the past thirty-five years have not altered the fact of continuing international competitiveness between Moscow and Washington. The 1980s will almost certainly show the same pattern of coexistential conflict as the past. See Graphic VI.

At all times civility and fair dealing toward all nations, including the USSR and the PRC, would be entirely in the U.S. interests. Confrontations would occur only if totalitarian states persisted in intervening in areas vital to leading nations in the U.S. alliance system. The United States would continue to try to resolve all conflicts peacefully, but it would not avoid confrontations by making concessions at the expense of its allies or its own objectives. This strategy would recommit the United States to the political and economic ideals in which most of its people believe. It is a coherent strategic concept for the 1980s around which the American people and their real friends abroad can rally.

GRAPHIC VI
U.S.-USSR Relations Since World War II

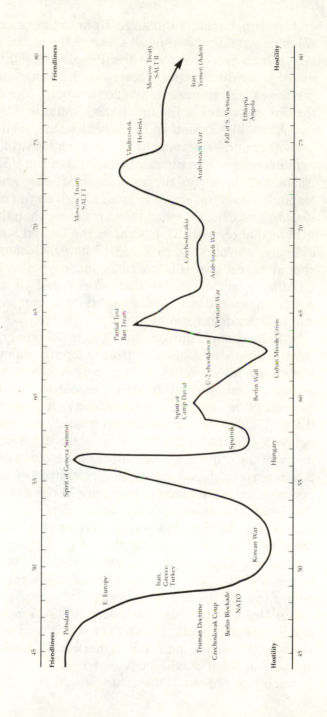

One firm benefit to emerge from creating an All-Oceans Alliance would be that in all areas of the globe, and even inside the Soviet Union and the People's Republic of China, many individuals would yearn for human rights, minority privileges, and representative government. The citizenry and the bureaucracies of the totalitarian states and their involuntary allies, like Poland and Czechoslovakia, realize that there is another and better way of life, less backward than the command economy and dictatorial politics of the USSR. Even the isolated Chinese on the mainland of Asia know that the "capitalist road" taken by Taiwan has given the citizens of the Republic of China a living standard more than three times as high as that of the PRC. Insofar as the United States takes the offensive beyond the confines of its All-Oceans Alliance, it should be only in this political and psychological sense of building a social model that works and of asserting the creativeness and material benefits of a comparatively free and independent form of society.

In the present configuration of world power, the United States could carry out the peacekeeping policy implicit in leading an All-Oceans league of cooperative nations with an annual expenditure of about 6 percent of its GNP, surely a bargain price for liberty and security. It is remarkable that the United States has now let its military share of GNP drop below 5 percent for the first time since the Korean war, and many of the other NATO countries are even lower, averaging 3 to 5 percent. Japan, likely to forge ahead of the USSR and become the second largest economy in the world as it enters the 1980s, still spends less than 1 percent of its GNP on military forces. Here is a great reservoir of economic strength for a navy and air force capable of protecting the sea-lanes around the Japanese home islands, while American naval forces shift the center of gravity of their concentration of power toward the South China Sea.

The United Kingdom, Germany (FRG), France, and Italy, at a minimum among the NATO nations, and preferably also Norway, Denmark, and the Netherlands, should offer to cooperate in what might be viewed as a peacekeeping constabulary of the sea. This effort would be quite apart from their NATO commitments for the defense of Europe against Soviet attack. The experience of the NATO navies in communications and maneuvers at sea with U.S. forces would be an invaluable North Atlantic anchor for the All-Oceans Alliance.

In the South Atlantic, Brazil would be the major sea power. With U.S. assistance, it might arrange for some kind of regional efforts in protecting the seas, cooperating with Argentina and Venezuela, and, on the Pacific coast, with Chile. This latter country, with its enormous coastline, is a natural seafaring state that in time may be able to join in South Pacific links connecting Latin America with Oceania and the Australia-Indonesia region.

None of these things will come about easily, but U.S. diplomacy marshalled in support of a clear-cut strategy of rallying the sea powers of the Free World to help one another would gradually rebuild confidence in the future through the vast reaches of the Atlantic and the Pacific.

A crucial move in the whole strategy would be the establishment of a major American naval presence in the Indian Ocean. For the immediate future the U.S. base would have to be on Diego Garcia, but most of the time, ships should be permitted to cruise as close to the Persian Gulf as possible. The United States should reinstate its plans for one more nuclear-powered supercarrier as a token of its intent to be supreme at sea. It probably should also transfer some of the fast carrier task forces from the Mediterranean to the Persian Gulf, where it would be in a better position to protect NATO interests than off the shores of Southern Europe.

For the period of maximum danger in 1982, consideration should also be given to supplementing our inadequate naval building program, which has been cut back from providing 600 combat ships to barely maintaining the present total of less than 400. Two of the *Essex* class aircraft carriers could be taken out of mothballs so they would supplement the Mediterranean and Indian Ocean forces. This measure is probably the only quick fix for increasing naval air strength where it is needed most—at the Suez end of the Mediterranean and near the Persian Gulf. While the *Essex* class carriers are obsolescent by modern U.S. standards, they are still fine fighting ships and are superior to the aircraft carriers the USSR is building. They certainly are adequate for showing the U.S. flag, working with other fleet elements to cover a substantial ocean or littoral area with firepower and airpower. They are also adequate for putting troops ashore in limited conventional military conflicts of the kind that may occur in East Africa or the Persian Gulf area.

For additional naval vessels of lesser combat capability but with shorter construction lead times, thought should also be given to placing orders in the excellent, now underemployed, shipyards in Japan and Taiwan if this is necessary to avoid overloading American facilities. In this way we could make up for lost time and very promptly begin to increase naval combat strength to something more like what was envisaged before the Carter administration's cuts in shipbuilding were made.

This effort to restore naval strength should be supplemented by comparable and supporting investments in aircraft, and especially in large numbers of long-range cruise missiles capable of being launched from land, at sea, or in the air. No provision of any arms limitation treaty should be entered into that might inhibit a crash program of deploying cruise missiles.

Probably an upgraded version of the FB-111 could be made available fairly soon, and plans should be made to supplement it with a new (post–B-1) manned bomber of maximum capability for penetration and cruise-missile launching.

While the development of a new, larger ICBM like the M-X is warranted, it could not affect the balance of military power much before 1990. For the present, maximum effort should be given to creating a *Minuteman II* force to be launched from wide-bodied civil-type aircraft and from vessels at sea, initially surface ships and later minisubmarines. We have the one-megaton warhead missiles now and could create a formidable mobile force quickly if the United States does not allow itself to be tied down by adverse provisions of the SALT II Treaty.

All of these military weapons are needed to provide muscle

for the All-Oceans Alliance but, of course, they will be of little value unless worldwide perceptions of U.S. strategy and national will change fairly rapidly. In this regard, Washington has much to do. The strategic thinking of the political leadership must be clarified, the diplomatic service must be rejuvenated, and a first-class intelligence system must be reestablished. In respect to this last item, the information derived from American photographic and remote-sensing reconnaissance satellites could be constituted as the Free World's peacekeeping data center. Sharing in the benefits of the ocean surveillance and economic survey capabilities of U.S. technical intelligence would be an effective incentive for nations to join the All-Oceans Alliance. All of these improvements in Washington's ability to handle foreign problems are necessary and desirable in any case, but they become imperative within the context of the alliance strategy.

After the disasters of the loss of Vietnam and the collapse of the Nixon presidency, the United States began to drift almost aimlessly in its strategic thinking. Gerald R. Ford, our only unelected president, performed competently and honestly, but he made no serious effort to define a new, comprehensive, postcontainment strategy for the United States. A clearer strategic concept was what the American people wanted and probably what they thought they would get when they elected Jimmy Carter by a narrow vote over Ford. In any event, they did not get it; the need is still there and still unfulfilled.

For three years American policy has aimed at pleasing everybody, including the USSR and the PRC, and has ended up losing credibility and prestige everywhere. It is plain that the United States cannot conduct its foreign and defense affairs much longer in such an unclear and often self-contradictory way—with what has been termed a policy of splendid oscillation. At the end of the 1970s President Carter's support in the public opinion polls reached an all-time low for the presidency—about 20 percent favorable.

What is needed now, however, is not so much a new face in the White House as a new strategy. The only one I can see as being positive and acceptable to both the U.S. and friendly nations abroad is a strategy of creating a peacetime league of trading states linked together in protection of the sea-lanes and one another. This strategy is not fundamentally anti-Soviet. It is simply pro-U.S. and pro-alliance. It is practicable and explicable in coherent ideas and plain words. Adoption of a strategy along the lines of bulding an All-Oceans Alliance in the 1980s is the only course that can deliver us from the extreme hazards of the 1982 period of maximum danger. Furthermore, this is the only way to give the country a psychological lift that would reverse the trend and correct the unfavorable tilt in the balance of power as it is now perceived and hence recorded in the assessment in this book.

With the twenty-two states suggested as partners of the United States in the All-Oceans Alliance it would have in its ranks concrete elements of perceived power $(C + E + M$ as calculated in Table 33) equal to more than half of the strength of the seventy-seven major nations of the world, three times the strength of Soviet-dominated politectonic Zone II, and more than twice the combined strength of Communist Asia, Zone III, and Zone II together. These assessments deal only with concrete elements of power and do not incorporate the factors of national strategy and national will $(S + W)$, since they are intangible and fluid and would change rapidly if a new and coherent strategy is adopted by the United States. Whenever American policymakers set forth a coherent strategy supported by an unfailing national will, the United States, alone or with a handful of allies, would be strong enough to stand firm against the USSR or the PRC or both. Actually each nation with which we firm up our security guarantees will serve as a peg tending to stabilize the immediate region around it. The militant ideological strategy of the totalitarian nations would be unable to succeed in tipping the balance of world power irretrievably in their favor.

In my view, no amount of charm and diplomacy nor any number of generous concessions can in the foreseeable future substantially alter the basic hostility of Peking and Moscow to the open societies. A coherent alliance-oriented strategy of the kind I have described will, however, be able to

Table 36. Strength of an All-Oceans Alliance by Politectonic Zones, 1978 (concrete elements of power)

Politectonic Zone	Country	Perceived Power Weights (C + E + M)	Zonal Total
I	United States	434	553
	Canada	87	
	Mexico	32	
IV	France	82	314
	Germany (FRG)	77	
	United Kingdom	68	
	Italy	48	
	Spain	39	
V	Egypt	38	127
	Turkey	36	
	Saudi Arabia	30	
	Israel	23	
VII	Indonesia	61	93
	Philippines	30	
	Singapore	2	
VIII	Japan	77	139
	Korea, South	33	
	China/Taiwan	29	
IX	Brazil	98	98
X	South Africa	36	57
	Zaire	21	
XI	Australia	73	89
	New Zealand	16	
	Total, United States plus 22 allied nations		1,470

202

GRAPHIC VII
Strength
of
Totalitarian and Free-World
Nations
(Concrete Elements of Power)
1978

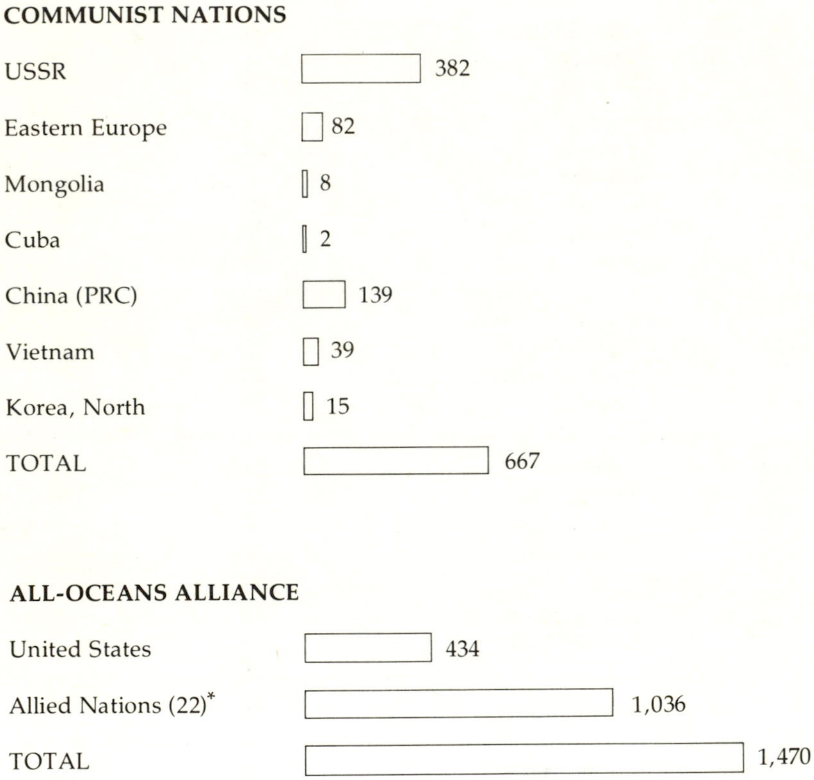

COMMUNIST NATIONS

USSR		382
Eastern Europe		82
Mongolia		8
Cuba		2
China (PRC)		139
Vietnam		39
Korea, North		15
TOTAL		667

ALL-OCEANS ALLIANCE

United States		434
Allied Nations (22)*		1,036
TOTAL		1,470

*The inner group of ten nations allied to the United States (Canada, United Kingdom, France, Germany (FRG), Italy, Japan, Australia, New Zealand, Israel, and China/Taiwan) account for over half of this concrete strength, i.e. 580 perceived power weights, as shown on Table XXXI. If the coefficients for strategy and will on Table XXXIII are taken into account, the strength of this inner group is even greater, i.e. 655 perceived power weights.

maintain the present rough equilibrium in international perceived power relationships. We have the capabilities to do it
as Table 36 and Graphic VII plainly show. Do we have the
clarity of vision and the will? I hope so.

In any case, in the face of revolutionary world disorders we
cannot relax in isolation and neutrality as we did in the
period before World War II. We must give first priority to
preserving the health and vigor of our open society, not in an
eventually beleaguered fortress North America, but across
the oceans within the structure of a strong, voluntary All-
Oceans Alliance.

Notes

Chapter One

1. Mahan, Alfred Thayer. *The Influence of Seapower Upon History.* New York: Hill and Wang, 1957.

2. The word "tectonic" literally means pertaining to construction or building, or specifically to the structural deformation of the earth's crust, whereby continental plates are gradually shifting relative to one another. For a more detailed discussion, see Walter Sullivan, *Continents in Motion*, as summarized in *The New York Magazine*, January 12, 1975.

3. We have included in this study 162 nations not under foreign jurisdiction. Of these, 149 are members of the United Nations. The non-UN nations are Andorra, China/Taiwan, Kiribati, North Korea, South Korea, Liechtenstein, Monaco, Nauru, San Marino, Switzerland, Tonga, Vatican City, and Zimbabwe-Rhodesia. Byelorussia and the Ukraine, both UN members, are treated within these pages as part of the Soviet Union.

Chapter Two

4. A periodic ranking and classification of nations along these lines, giving slightly more severe ratings to some nations than I do, is published annually by Freedom House under the title "Freedom at Issue." See the January–February 1978 Special Issue, no. 44.

Chapter Three

5. All figures on population in this chapter are taken from the

National Basic Intelligence Factbook. Washington, D.C.: Superinten-
dent of Documents, January 1979. They are the latest reliable,
mutually comparable statistics available. The volume is available
from Document Expediting (DOCEX) Project, Library of Congress,
Washington, D.C. 20540.

6. *Ibid.* (*The Factbook* for July 1976 gives territory in square
miles.)

Chapter Four

7. The 1978 GNP figures have been calculated from a variety of
sources. For the United States, the USSR, the countries of the Soviet
bloc, West Europe, and Asia they have been taken from statistics
appearing in a Department of State report by Dr. Herbert Block and
from the *International Financial Statistics* published by the International Monetary Fund, July 1979, vol. 32, no. 7. For the countries of
Latin America calculations have been made on the basis of com-
puter printouts furnished by the Organization of American States as
well as the IMF *International Financial Statistics*, July 1979. GNP
figures for the Arab nations have been calculated on the basis of per
capita GNP figures provided by the Arab regional desk of the
World Bank. Figures for New Zealand, Bangladesh, Malaysia, and
Israel have been obtained from the Department of State reports by
Dr. Block.

8. *The Oil and Gas Journal*, December 25, 1978, and the *British
Petroleum Statistical Review of the World Oil Industry*, 1978.

9. *International Coal 1977*. Washington, D.C.: National Coal
Association and Coal Exporters Association of the United States,
Inc., 1978. Based on the analysis of the 1975 figures, liquid fuels ac-
counted for 44 percent of world energy consumption, solid fuels for
33 percent, and the remaining 23 percent was provided by hydro,
nuclear, and imported electricity. Bituminous and anthracite coal
are included. The source for estimated production figures was the
Geographical Statistics Unit of the U.S. Bureau of Mines; net ex-
port/import data were also supplied by the U.S. Bureau of Mines.

10. Natural gas figures were calculated from raw data supplied
by the U.S. Department of Energy and by the U.S Bureau of Mines.

11. Preliminary data for nuclear power were supplied by the
U.S. Department of Energy, Uranium Resources and Enrichment
Division, Resources Application, Washington, D.C., July 1979.

12. Production of iron ore in 1978 was supplied by the Office of
Geographic Statistics, U.S. Bureau of Mines; net export/import data

were also supplied by the Bureau of Mines.

13. Copper production in 1978 was supplied by the U.S. Bureau of Mines. Net export/import figures were calculated from figures made available by the Office of Geographic Statistics, U.S. Bureau of Mines.

14. *Ibid.*

15. *Ibid.*

16. *Ibid.*

17. The preferred measure is probably the proportion of GNP made up by the manufacture of machines and machine tools. These products especially measure the capacity of the economy to rejuvenate itself (i.e., replace industrial capacity as it wears out) and to expand. Unfortunately, comparative data for this component of manufacturing are not readily available.

18. United Nations. *Monthly Bulletin of Statistics* (hereinafter referred to as UN *MBS*), June 1979. Yearly rates were extrapolated where necessary. China (PRC) estimate was supplied by U.S Bureau of Mines.

19. UN *MBS*, June 1979. Yearly rates were extrapolated where necessary. USSR estimate was supplied by the U.S. Bureau of Mines.

20. UN *MBS*, June 1979. Yearly rates were extrapolated where necessary. Estimates for the PRC and France were supplied by U.S. Bureau of Mines.

21. U.S. Department of Agriculture. *Foreign Agricultural Circulars*, FG-7-77 and FG-4-78.

22. UN *MBS*, June 1979, and IMF *International Financial Statistics*, July 1979. Import figures for the United Arab Emirates and Iraq were extrapolated from figures covering the period January to September 1978. Figures for Rumania and Bulgaria were extrapolated from annual figures covering the years 1974 to 1977.

Chapter Five

23. Von Clausewitz, Carl. *On War*. London and Boston: Routledge & Kegan Paul, 1968, vol. 1, pp. 2, 23.

24. Data for this chapter were taken primarily from Annual Reports by Secretaries of Defense or Chairmen of the Joint Chiefs of Staff. The overall analysis and some details are based on a special unpublished research report prepared for use in this book by Edward N. Luttwak. It also draws upon Dr. Luttwak's *Strategic Power: Military Capabilities and Political Utility*. Washington, D.C.: The

Center for Strategic and International Studies, Georgetown University, 1976.

25. U.S. Department of State. *SALT II, Senate Testimony,* July 9–11, 1979, p. 35.

26. Donley, Michael B., ed. *The SALT Handbook,* Washington, D.C.: The Heritage Foundation, 1979, pp. 62, 75.

27. *SALT II, Senate Testimony,* p. 34.

28. U.S. Department of Defense. *Annual Report, Fiscal Year 1979,* February 1978, p. 47.

29. The International Institute of Strategic Studies. *The Military Balance 1978–1979,* p. 79.

30. Data provided by the program analysis unit of the Department of Defense, *New York Times,* June 19, 1979, p. A 12, and *SALT II, Senate Testimony,* July 9–11, 1979, p. 35.

31. The strategic capability of the *Backfire* is a question of some controversy. The *Military Balance* lists the *Backfire* as having an unrefueled range of 5,500 miles, clearly a figure with some strategic implications.

Chapter Six

32. *The Military Balance 1977–1978,* p. 8, and John M. Collins: *American and Soviet Military Trends Since the Cuban Missile Crisis.* Washington, D.C.: The Center for Strategic and International Studies, Georgetown University, 1978, p. 50.

33. Sources for these figures vary. Data for the USSR, Egypt, Israel, and North Korea are taken from *The Military Balance 1978–1979.* The PRC estimate was obtained by comparing the 1978 defense expenditures in *The Military Balance 1978–1979* (US $23–28 billion) with the PRC's GNP of 1976. Iran, Turkey, and Iraq figures were computed using expenditures listed in *The Military Balance 1978–1979.* The figure for Syria was computed by adjusting the 1975 GNP to 1978 (using 4 percent growth) and 1978 defense expenditures from *The Military Balance 1978–1979.* Because of the difficulty of obtaining actual defense expenditures, these figures should be viewed as orders of magnitude.

Chapter Seven

34. Many of the citations in this section of the chapter are from a Miami University monograph by Foy D. Kohler, et al. *Soviet*

Strategy for the Seventies, 1973. The interpretation of Soviet doctrine presented here corresponds closely with the findings of Ambassador Kohler and his colleagues.

35. *New York Times,* February 25, 1976.

36. Foreign Broadcast Information Service. *People's Republic of China,* December 12, 1978. (Hereinafter referred to as FBIS-CHINA.)

37. These quotations are from Mao's works found in *Quotations from Chairman Mao Tse-tung.* Peking: Foreign Languages Press, 1966 (First Edition).

38. FBIS-CHINA, Thursday, September 1, 1977, p. 65.

39. *Peking Review,* October 6, 1978, no. 40, p. 6.

40. *Ibid.,* June 22, 1979, no. 25, p. 16.

41. *Washington Post,* March 25, 1979.

42. Peking Review, July 6, 1979, no. 27, p. 30.

43. The Department of State, News Release, May 22, 1977.

44. *Ibid.,* March 16, 1978.

45. *Ibid.,* March 1979, no. 57.

46. *Washington Star,* March 16, 1979.

47. *New York Times,* July 26, 1979.

Chapter Eight

48. Lippmann, Walter. *U.S. Foreign Policy.* London: Hamish Hamilton, 1943, p. 4.

Index